S. SHAKTHIDHARAN is a western Sydney storyteller with Sri Lankan heritage and Tamil ancestry. Shakthi is a writer, director and producer of theatre and film, and composer of original music. His debut play *Counting and Cracking* (Belvoir and Co-Curious) received community, commercial and critical acclaim at the 2019 Sydney and Adelaide Festivals. The script won the Victorian Premier's Literature Prize and the NSW Premier's Nick Enright Prize for Playwriting; the production won seven Helpmann and three Sydney Theatre awards. Shakthi is the Artistic Director of Kurinji and Artistic Lead at Co-Curious. Co-Curious is a sister company to award-winning community arts company CuriousWorks, where Shakthi was the Founder and Artistic Director from 2003 to 2018. Shakthi was the inaugural Carriageworks Associate Artist, a Belvoir Associate Artist and is a recipient of both the Philip Parsons and Kirk Robson awards.

Left to right: Nipuni Sharada, Hazem Shammas, Monroe Reimers, Jay Emmanuel and Ahi Karunaharan in the Belvoir/Co-Curious production of Counting and Cracking. *Photo: Brett Boardman.*

COUNTING & CRACKING

எண்ணிக்கை, இல்லையேல் கையோங்கு

ගණන් නොගන්නේ නම් ගණන් කරන්න

S. SHAKTHIDHARAN

ASSOCIATE WRITER: EAMON FLACK

CURRENCY PRESS
The performing arts publisher

CURRENCY PLAYS

First published in 2019 by Company B, Pty Ltd
This revised edition first published in 2020
by Currency Press Pty Ltd,
Gadigal Land, Suite 310, 46–56 Kippax Street, Surry Hills, NSW 2010, Australia
enquiries@currency.com.au
www.currency.com.au

Typeset by Integral for Currency Press.
Cover design by Lisa White for Currency Press.
Author photo by Ken Leanfore courtesy of Belvoir.

Currency Press acknowledges the Traditional Owners of the Country on which we live and work. We pay our respects to all Aboriginal and Torres Strait Islander Elders, past and present.

Contents

Playwright's note

Ten years ago I was hungry. Hungry to learn about my mother's homeland. To know my history. So I started on a journey that had no clear end.

I read everything there was to read on the subject. I had conversations with so many gracious and intelligent Sri Lankans from all around the world. I was reeling from the overload, but slowly, very slowly, a story was being born. It was a story about parents and children. About coming together and breaking apart and coming together again—in our families, our governments, our countries.

And this story became something bigger than my own hunger. It became something that had a power. The power to help my mother reconcile with her homeland. To connect people across deep divides. The power to collapse time and join continents.

The story became less about fitting my community into a simple narrative, and more about presenting a group of people in all their glorious complexity. It became less about discovering 'the truth' of what happened in Sri Lanka, or what brought us to Australia, and more about understanding the stage as a sacred space where many truths can gather at once.

The stories we choose to believe in underlie all our actions, thoughts and feelings. In *Counting and Cracking* I hope to provide readers with a new story to believe in: about Australia; about Sri Lanka.

It's a story in which migrants are not asked to discard parts of themselves to fit in, but instead are asked to present their full selves, to expand our idea of what this country can be.

It's a story of how the politics of division can win the battle, but never the war, around how power is gained in this world.

It's a story in which love may not triumph over adversity, but through sheer persistence and resilience can eventually overcome it.

And finally it's a story about reconciliation: between parents and children, between neighbours and enemies, between your new home and your old home, between society and its institutions.

Counting and Cracking is dedicated to Lingamani Rajarayan (1933-2018), affectionately known to me as Chinni. Chinni was the first person in my family to open up to me about Sri Lanka. We sat in her kitchen in London and over several days of Scrabble and curry she talked and I listened. Her spirit is woven into the fabric of this story. My only disappointment in the making of this work is that Chinni is not here to see it.

Counting and Cracking features direct quotes from a diverse array of people: Sri Lankan politician (and mathematician) C. Suntharalingam (with the permission of his family), Sri Lankan journalist Lasantha Wickrematunge (with the permission of his brother Lal), Yolngu woman and artist (and dear friend) Rosealee Pearson (with the permission of her family), and my mother Anandavalli. *Counting and Cracking* is a work of fiction and there is no intention for any of its characters to represent or reference anyone in real life. Nevertheless, real life has occasionally worked its way into the story, as it almost always does.

Anjalendran is an architect and my great aunt's son. We sat at his dining table in the first house he built—his own home, in Colombo. Over lamprais and Chindian takeaway we read aloud my great-grandfather's public articles and private letters. These were bold and confronting missives. Anjalendran's resulting frank and honest thoughts on our troubled history did not diminish his pride or sense of belonging to Sri Lanka. I continue to be inspired by his fearless approach to a truthful reconciliation with our past.

Anushya took my wife and I to Jaffna before my mother was ready to go back there. To go to Jaffna for the first time is like an exhalation. There is an impossible amount of expectation before your arrival, and then a slow release as you cross over to the peninsula. You witness a region that is re-building and re-imagining itself, and amidst all that you glimpse the remains of the life that your family once had, long ago. The temple they once helped build and now only donate to. Their old home with its new occupiers. It was on this trip that I first started to understand our ancestral homeland and the fullness of the Sri Lankan picture. Anushya guided us through this complexity with endless patience and a quiet, deep intelligence.

My mother did not talk to me about Sri Lanka in any deep way for the first 30-odd years of my life. She had closed her heart to the country. She has witnessed the development of this work—been a quiet presence for many of the research conversations, attended each of the readings and the showings. The process of making this work has changed her. She is reconciling with her homeland, and has started talking about Ceylon again. In doing so, she has made the choice to be vulnerable. I am grateful for that. It is the hard choice, but we are immeasurably better for it, as artistic collaborators on this project, and as mother and son.

My wife Aimée is the only other person who has known about this play since the beginning. She has seen it as a series of placards pasted up on the wall of a little hut in Tasmania. She has seen all the alternate versions that no-one else will ever see. She knew what this work could be before I did. It is through her I found the confidence to write a story like this.

There are many other people who can't be mentioned publicly—people who would be labelled things like bureaucrats or prisoners, but who spoke to me with a sense of shared humanity across all of society, no matter their individual position. These people shared at length their most private thoughts and I can only hope that I have adequately honoured their generosity with this story.

A number of unusual and unlikely opportunities were strung together to make writing a work like this a possibility. The years of research and the first scenes were supported through an Australia Council for the Arts Young Artists Initiative grant in 2008—an opportunity that is no longer available. The first drafts were written during my time as Associate Artist at Carriageworks, where absolutely no restrictions were put on what I might do with my time there, from 2013 to 2015.

But the infrastructure of an independent artist alone cannot support a work of this size. From 2011 to 2019 *Counting and Cracking* was shepherded by CuriousWorks and Co-Curious, forming a part of their artistic program. It is a long time to have a work in development—but without that kind of longevity works like this simply cannot happen.

Since 2013 Eamon Flack and the Belvoir team have done everything in their power to make this story reach our mainstage, including amassing an incredible group of philanthropic supporters. They did not try to change this work to fit into pre-existing structures. Instead they took a leap of faith to make something new, in a new way.

It's been quite the ride for all of us. Each member in this new coalition has utilised their different sets of expertise to make this wildly ambitious dream a reality. None of us could have done it on our own. Much like the story of *Counting and Cracking*, the process of making this work proves that real power can be gained when different groups come together to create something new.

S. Shakthidharan
Sydney 2020

To read some responses to the first production of *Counting and Cracking* from members of the Sri Lankan community, visit the Kurinji website:
https://kurinji.com.au/counting-and-cracking-community-response/

Director's note

This is an Australian story. It's not only an Australian story, but it is definitely an Australian story. Much of it takes place in Sri Lanka: the story of Australia is the story of many places, many people. Ours is a migrant nation on Aboriginal land. At its best it is a land of refuge and new beginnings. With each successive wave of arrivals, from the earliest times to the English boats to now, the country has changed, and the national story has changed. *Counting and Cracking* is a new offer to that big unfolding story.

It is about many things, but at its heart is the fundamental need every one of us has to connect to each other, the world, the past, and the future. Most of our lives are spent making and nurturing these connections. We do this on every scale of life, in small ways and big ways. The small ways are usually age-old, closely held things—love, family, language, story, belief, food, home, the passage of time from one generation to the next. The big ways are more likely to be newer, more modern, more public inventions—the big shared narratives of national identity, political negotiation, economic purpose. *Counting and Cracking* is about the relationship between the big stuff and the small stuff, and what happens when the big stuff tears apart the small stuff. A language shattered, a family torn apart, a place torn down— these things are fragile. They cannot be taken for granted. We inherit them, they are in our keeping. The big stuff must take care of the small stuff. The small stuff is what matters most. We cannot be a nation or a whole person if we cannot keep hold of these connections. And when a person or a group of people have been torn apart then the only thing to do is to begin again—to revive the old connections, or make new ones. Fortunately, new connections are always possible. New stories are always possible. We mix from here and there, from now and the past. Water and water.

This show was the product of new connections. Bringing it together took an almighty effort by a great coalition of people from many walks of life. Belvoir could not have done this without Co-Curious, and

Co-Curious could not have done this without Belvoir. We each had to discover what we did and didn't know, and what the other knew that we didn't. Step by step, through days then weeks then years of conversation, we began to see that this show was not just necessary, it was also possible. Then we had to convince a lot of other people that it was necessary and possible. We had to find new partners, new collaborators. Most people were willing—not all, but most. We travelled around Australia. We travelled to London, Delhi, Bangalore, Chennai, Singapore, Kuala Lumpur. We spoke to people in Paris, Wellington, Toronto, New York. We travelled all around Sri Lanka, from Colombo to Jaffna to Kayts to Batticaloa. Little by little the coalition of people and organisations grew. Together it took our two companies almost six years to bring everything into alignment, and it has only been possible because hundreds of people from all over Australia and around the world have joined in.

Eamon Flack
Sydney 2020

Introduction

Radhika Coomaraswamy

Silence. It is usually the first response to violence, humiliation and trauma. Radha, the chief protagonist of S. Shakthidharan's play *Cracking and Counting*, has been silent for 20 years. She will not tell her son Siddhartha what took place and why she left Sri Lanka in 1983, and the nature of the unspoken passion that keeps her wedded to a country and a people who appear to have betrayed her. Having found freedom and a new life, she brings up a caring and loving son, who will be an Australian first but will also long for a deeper understanding of his roots and the DNA of his existence.

Siddhartha understands that his mother has made the choice to be vulnerable. Having left Sri Lanka apparently widowed, pregnant and alone, she has never remarried and has kept her family and her values together. She did not take short cuts or adopt false gods. She created a home for the creativity of her child; a home open to the world while deeply anchored in Asian traditions. She did not take an easy path to security, just relied on hard work and a good heart. Her son is her legacy.

From the late 1970s, Tamil discourse emanating from Sri Lanka increasingly became fraught with anger, hate and intolerance. The riots of 1983 became the intense focal point of Tamil identity. The sense of grievance and victimhood carried the world over by fleeing asylum seekers and migrants saw the rise of militarism within Sri Lanka and the unspoken communal duty of no compromise with the Sinhalese.

Voices of compassion and humanism that could have given direction to the violence and suffering of the Sri Lankan Tamil community were forsaken, erased or assassinated. The beauty of this play is that it finally evokes that voice—the muted voice of humanism—and brings it centrestage. At its core, the play reminds us of the interconnectedness of the world and the universal struggles for justice and rights.

The 1983 riots are central to Sri Lankan Tamil identity. The political scientist and historian Benedict Anderson writes of how many groups are held together by memories of collective victimhood and trauma. For Sri Lankan Tamils, 1983 and the end of the war in 2009 often define the way they interact with the world. The year 1983 has been erased within Sri Lanka, forgotten by the vast majority of Sinhalese. The refusal to commemorate or retell the events of that year has effectively wiped out the memory from their point of view. But for Sri Lankan Tamils, especially those who fled overseas, it remains central. For many of those over 35 years of age, it has come to define the contours of who they are.

This definition of who one is when it comes to traumatic events can come in terms of increasing militancy, strident agitation and a withdrawal into an exclusive identity. Alternatively, it can be an act of reconciliation, looking deeply into our wounds with the hope of healing. *Counting and Cracking* is perhaps the most heroic example of the latter approach. The main theme of the play is reconciliation through truth telling. It is epic in scale, pulling together a diverse cast of characters and disparate scenes to weave a story of atonement and recovery. At the end of the play you feel you have lived through the emotions of a whole historic era.

Funerals have become an awkward moment in the lives of Sri Lankan Tamils living in Sri Lanka or abroad. It is therefore fitting that the play opens with Radha and her son Siddhartha on the banks of the Georges River, attempting to scatter the ashes of Radha's recently deceased mother. Ironically, Radha remembers that she fled Sri Lanka in 1983 with the ashes of her precious grandfather, fresh from cremation and placed inside a Tupperware box. She has yet to dispose of them. During the heyday of Sri Lankan Tamil existence, before 1983, funerals and weddings would mean hundreds of people gathering together. Managing such crowds was part of the rituals a young girl had to learn.

The scene is very different now. There are only three people at the Georges River funeral—the priest, Radha and Siddhartha. The priest asks that a male from the family accompany Siddhartha into the water to throw the ashes. 'There is no-one,' Radha says. The priest insists. Radha is equally adamant, so the priest relents and the ceremony takes place. While Sri Lankan Tamil funerals abroad in the larger cities sometimes draw the diaspora community together, Sri Lankan Tamil funerals in Colombo now have barely enough people to carry the coffin or be pallbearers. The opportunity to mourn, grieve and recover, either as individuals, families or a collective has so radically transformed.

As Siddhartha throws the ashes into the river, he sees the grander vision of water mixing with water. When he confesses his love to his Aboriginal girlfriend Lily, and they reflect on the lack of interconnectedness between their realities, he remembers the water. They reflect on how the water carrying the ashes of Siddhartha's grandmother would inevitably make its way and mix with the waters of Yirrkala, Lily's homeland. The mixing and the incessant flow is the universe's answer to our constant bickering and parochialism.

The play, though deeply inquisitive about Sri Lankan reality, is finally about the fluidity and hybridity of identity itself. It is a grand vision that highlights our roots as well as our contradictions. Despite all the tensions, Radha's grandmother wanted her to marry the Sinhalese son of her father's best friend. Radha infuriated her grandparents by marrying the son of a fruit seller, now an engineer, who was of a different Tamil caste. That radical choice and the negative reaction of Radha's family to it—'marriage is the coming together of two families'—reminds us that diversity practically always comes with resistance.

The intensity of communal conflict is set against the omnipresence of multiculturalism. Siddhartha's name is Buddhist though his parents are Hindu. Radha sings 'thevarams' to Siddhartha on their balcony in Sydney and he muses when he is older that his identity was not only 'mustard seeds and curry leaves' but also 'salty air and beer'. Siddhartha's clothes are always a mixture of east and west. The play is full of the rich and dynamic interaction of cultures. It is water constantly flowing. Lily, Siddhartha's girlfriend, says she had a DNA test done and that part of her is Sri Lankan. Muslim neighbours sharing Ramadan feasts, and Turkish air conditioner installers seeking romantic dates fill the pages of this play with multi-ethnicity like breathing fresh air after you have been caught in a tunnel.

A towering figure in the play, obviously based on the life of the playwright's own family member, is Apah, Radha's grandfather, who brings her up while her parents are abroad. This larger than life, lion-hearted character was a professor of mathematics, a graduate of Cambridge University and a cabinet member of the present Parliament.

'From the paddy field to the algebraic equation', he symbolises the Sri Lankan intellectuals and politicians who brought us independence. Contentious, vociferous and performative, they move away from consensus building to open conflict and direct challenge. While his friend and cabinet colleague Vinsanda drifts toward dictatorship in trying to deal with the JVP insurrection, Apah strongly resists all attempts to compromise democracy. It is inevitable that he would die of a broken heart in 1983.

The description of Apah's political actions brings nostalgia for the politics of another era, one where filibustering in Parliament, satyagrahas at the Galle Face Green, handcuffing yourself to chairs to prevent eviction by the Speaker of Parliament and other forms of non-violent, direct protest were the mainstay of the political imagination. The play has many such epic scenes. All that changed in the 1970s when violence made its entrance. The politicians of independence who saw politics as cricket—'see you at the crease', says Visandha as he leaves Apah's company—are now dismissed by latter-day youth as patrons of privilege, lacking connection to the vast majority of the poor and the underprivileged who make up Sri Lanka's population.

No play featuring Sri Lankan Tamils can be authentic if it does not have an honest conversation about Tamil militancy and extremism. Radha's husband Thirru's sister, Swathi, having seen one of her friends killed in a crackdown, runs off and joins the female wing of the Tamil Tigers. As we watch counterterrorism strategies unfold throughout the world we know that if a family member is found to belong to an extremist group all members are under a cloud. Thirru, Radha's husband, who has no truck with Tamil militancy, is nevertheless arrested and disappears. Radha is told he was killed in the riots. Having heard the news, she leaves Sri Lanka with her unborn baby, a few items of clothing and her grandfather's ashes. Thirru reappears at the end of the play, fleeing his captors. Desperate to find asylum in Australia and reunite with his family, he connects with Radha and her son. Radha remembers this recent history all too well. When fundraisers for the Tigers appear and mention her grandfather she says: 'Do not mention him in the same breath as the Tigers. Even the Gods will not forgive you for what you are doing.'

The portrayal of Sinhalese characters in this play is with affection.

Like the Tamils they live with the undercurrent of violence, a violence of great complexity. Nihinsa, the domestic aid, is a central character of the story. Her drama on the sidelines of the play gives us a sense of how unreal the life of the elites were. Her son attacks the Kataragama police station as a member of the JVP, a Sinhalese Marxist rebel group. The desperation of the life of poor Sinhalese is represented by Nihinsa and enacted through this side drama. Her husband is given a 12-year prison sentence. To protect her family, Nihinsa requests her son, Maithri, join the army. Swathi, Radha's sister-in-law, and Maithri are seen attacking each other in a mimed battle scene.

Despite all the violence, what finally emerges between the main Sinhalese and Tamil characters in the play, is a deeper understanding and common struggles though waged in a parallel universe. The Sinhalese hero in the play is Hasa, whose bravery mirrors that of one of Sri Lanka's leading journalists. In love with Radha but turned best friend, he facilitates both Radha's and Thirru's departure from Sri Lanka. As a fearless journalist, he is finally killed, and Radha and her family deeply mourn his passing. In fact as the backdrop of Sri Lanka's modern history unfolds in this play, we see many of these characters as heroes holding steadfast to certain values as they experience the bloody and nasty vicissitudes of life.

The portrayal of the women in *Counting and Cracking* is also inspiring. Radha, Aacha, Swathi, Nihinsa are all women with agency who play a decisive part in the lives of the people around them. None of them are part of the décor. Grandmother Aacha is no subservient Sita but one who commands her politician husband in many important decisions that affect private life. Radha, the mathematician, gives up her chance to enter Cambridge, defies her grandparents and marries a Tamil of a different caste. Swathi joins the Tigers. Though a cog in the Tiger wheel she is empowered, although her acts of willfulness will destroy her brother and her family. Nihinsa, having to cope with the frailty and folly of her family while working full-time in someone else's home, is the quiet and strong force that negotiates her family's future by urging her son to join the army. These women are strong and decisive. Lily, Siddhartha's love interest, though, is the way of the future; an Aboriginal woman, at peace with herself, caring and nurturing, willing to cross society's barriers in pursuit of her dreams.

Counting and Cracking also gives us a glimpse into that subterranean world where migrants, undocumented workers, people smugglers, asylum seekers and trafficked victims traverse the world of desperation and pain. Some are stateless, belonging to no-one, having to survive on wit and cunning. They live with false passports and visas and are kept in containers and dark rooms for days on end by human smugglers. Thirru decides to flee Sri Lanka and is taken to Mannar, Rameshwaram, Malaysia, Indonesia and then finally to Australia. We get a glimpse of this subterranean world through his transit.

Political values and frameworks hover over the play, though humanity trumps their certainty. The play has full-hearted support for the values of democracy but a scepticism about its practices. 'Democracy means the counting of heads within limits and the cracking of heads beyond those limits,' says Apah in describing the politics of his time. This play is about going 'beyond those limits' when systems of democracy break down and are overwhelmed by violence. Violence brings another discourse. The focus shifts from democracy to human rights. The young Radha clutches and reads reports by Amnesty International. There is a subtle understanding in the play that these political values are not shared values; they are in fact very precious and need to be protected and fought for.

Art in Sri Lanka cannot get away from these debates and discussions. The great artists of contemporary Sri Lanka, Jagath Weerasinghe, Sanathanan and Thenuwara have directly faced the political and moral dilemmas arising from years of war and conflict. Shakthidharan is also in this category. Silence is first broken through art. It captures the sentiments and the nuances. It gives first expression to the rainbow of emotions. Through the work of these artists a country expresses its pain and suffering.

But there is also lightness and hope. That is why *Counting and Cracking* is a superlative play. The give, take and repartee between the characters is much of the play and the tension does not lift for a minute. The play is also full of mime, music, dance and playfulness that allow one to experience the plotline within a rich context. One is totally engrossed. So it is not only a play about epic events but also a display of literary craftsmanship, both subtle and extraordinary, depending on the event and the scene.

One cannot get away from the fact that this play is mainly about passion, the passion the characters of all ethnicities have for Sri Lanka. It has been a turbulent passion that has ripped the country apart as everyone tries to lay claim to it. Twenty-one years after she left Sri Lanka, 20 years after her silence, Radha mentions to Siddhartha that she wants to go back to Sri Lanka and take the Tupperware box full of her grandfather's ashes to scatter them in her waters. 'I loved Sri Lanka. I still do. Not just the people, but the land itself. I miss it. Every day.'

In such a context this play is essentially about the hunger for reconciliation, a yearning for forgiveness, remorse and closure—a closure that is strongly resisted by many vested interests. Perhaps the Sinhalese jailor who tortures Thirru in the play because his parents were killed in a Tiger bomb blast reflects our contradictions. He will not forgive. The mere presence of Thirru infuriates him. But he loves Muralitharan, Sri Lanka's iconic Tamil cricketer. He cheers him on and feels at one with him. The jailor reminds Sri Lankans that we live with these contradictions on a daily basis. While we exclude the other, she also lives inside.

Finally the play, despite its intense Sri Lankan focus, will remain with every single member of the audience. Universality is the bottom line of *Counting and Cracking*, building on a common humanity. The coming together of Siddhartha and Lily, the Aboriginal reality with Sri Lanka's forgotten child, both dreaming of the place where the waters inevitably mix, reminds us of our interconnectedness. But it is interconnectedness with a moral core. It is a cast of mostly heroes clutching important values. They are thrown about in different directions, constantly being tested. Yet they retain their common humanity. They are looking for transcendence. As Hasa writes, 'There is a calling that is above high office, fame, money or security. It is the call of the conscience.'

Sri Lanka

July 2020

Radhika Coomaraswamy was a former Under Secretary General of the United Nations and Special Representative on Children and Armed Conflict.

Counting and Cracking was first co-produced by Belvoir Street
Theatre and Co-Curious Ltd, and developed with the support of
CuriousWorks, at Sydney Town Hall on 11 January 2019, with the
following cast:

RADHA	Nadie Kammallaweera
SIDDHARTHA	Shiv Palekar
APAH	Prakash Belawadi
AACHA / DHAMAYANTHI /	
OLD NIHINSA	Sukania Venugopal
THIRRU	Antonythasan Jesuthasan
YOUNG RADHA	Vaishnavi Suryaprakash
YOUNG THIRRU	Jay Emmanuel
NIHINSA	Nipuni Sharada
HASANGA	Nicholas Brown
VINSANDA	Monroe Reimers
LILY	Rarriwuy Hick
BALA / MAITHRI	Rajan Velu
SUNIL	Ahilan Karunaharan
PRIEST	Gandhi MacIntyre
ISMET	Hazem Shammas
SWATHI	Monica Kumar
BAND	Kranthi Kiran Mudigonda
	Janakan Raj
	Venkhatesh Sritharan

Director, Eamon Flack
Associate Director, S. Shakthidharan
Cultural and Costume Advisor, Anandavalli
Set and Costume Designer, Dale Ferguson
Lighting Designer, Damien Cooper
Sound Designer and Composer, Stefan Gregory

Associate Sound Designer, Jessica Dunn
Movement and Fight Director, Nigel Poulton
Accent Coach, Linda Nicholls-Gidley
Assistant Director, Carissa Licciardello
Associate Artist, Suzanne Pereira
Stage Manager, Luke McGettigan
Deputy Stage Manager, Jennifer Parsonage
Assistant Stage Manager, Julia Orlando

Translations
Tamil, Kulasegaram Sanchayan
Sinhala, Nadya Perera and Nadie Kammallaweera
With the support of Ahilan Karunaharan and Nipuni Sharada

Counting and Cracking was developed with the support of CuriousWorks and Belvoir St Theatre. The author would also like to acknowledge the support of Carriageworks, Playwriting Australia, the Australian Government through the Australia Council for the Arts and the NSW Government through Create NSW.

MAIN CHARACTERS

SIDDHARTHA, an arts and media studies student
RADHA, Siddhartha's mother (amma), a mathematician
DHAMAYANTHI, Siddhartha's grandmother (ammamma)
APAH, Siddhartha's great-grandfather, a politician
AACHA, Siddhartha's great-grandmother

LILY, Siddhartha's girlfriend, a law student

THIRRU, Siddhartha's father, an engineer
BALA, Thirru's father, a fruit seller from Jaffna
SWATHI, Thirru's sister

NIHINSA, Apah and Aacha's housekeeper
MAITHRI, Nihinsa's son

VINSANDA, personal friend, political enemy of Apah
HASANGA, Vinsanda's son, a journalist

COMPLETE CHARACTER LIST

All characters speak English unless otherwise indicated.

ACT ONE

PRIEST, 90s (Tamil-speaking Sri Lankan)
SIDDHARTHA, 20
RADHA, 48 (Tamil- and Singhalese-speaking Sri Lankan)
LILY, early 20s (Yolngu Matha-speaking Australian)
ISMET (Arabic-speaking Turkish Australian)
FUNDRAISER (Tamil-speaking Sri Lankan)
JAILOR (Singhalese-speaking Sri Lankan, broken English)
THIRRU, 48 (Tamil- and Singhalese-speaking Sri Lankan)

CRICKET COMMENTATOR (Australian)

CRICKET COMMENTATOR (Sri Lankan)

ISMET'S SON

SUNIL, 60s (Tamil-speaking Indian)

OLD NIHINSA, 70s (Singhalese-speaking Sri Lankan, broken English)

HASA, 50s (Singhalese-speaking Sri Lankan)

POLICEMAN 1 (Singhalese-speaking Sri Lankan, broken English)

TEENAGE RADHA

TEENAGE THIRRU

NIHINSA, 20s

APAH, 80s (Tamil- and Singhalese-speaking Sri Lankan)

ACT TWO

NIHINSA, 20s

APAH, 50s

PRIEST, 50s

DHAMAYANTHI, 20s (Tamil- and Singhalese-speaking Sri Lankan)

AACHA, 50s (Tamil- and Singhalese-speaking Sri Lankan)

BABY RADHA

BALA, 20s (Tamil-speaking Sri Lankan, broken English)

VINSANDA, 50s (Singhalese-speaking Sri Lankan)

SIDDHARTHA, 20

RADHA, 48

HASA, 50s

THIRRU, 48

SUNIL, 60s

NIHINSA, 40s

AACHA, 70s

MALE SERVANT (Singhalese-speaking Sri Lankan, no English)
HOPPER MAN (Tamil-speaking Sri Lankan, no English)
YOUNG WOMAN (Tamil- and Singhalese-speaking Sri Lankan)
YOUNG HASA, 20s
YOUNG THIRRU, 22
SWATHI, teenager (Tamil-speaking Sri Lankan, broken English)
SUNIL, 30s
BRIDE (Singhalese-speaking Sri Lankan)
ARIF (Tamil-speaking Sri Lankan)
YOUNG RADHA, 22
MISTER LEVI
MAITHRI, 20s (Singhalese-speaking Sri Lankan, no English)
APAH, 70s
VINSANDA, 70s
POLICEMAN 2 (Singhalese-speaking Sri Lankan, no English)
WEDDING GUESTS
BYSTANDER 1 (Tamil-speaking Sri Lankan, broken English)
BYSTANDER 2 (Singhalese-speaking Sri Lankan)
BYSTANDER 3 (Tamil- and Singhalese-speaking Sri Lankan)
LILY, early 20s
TAMIL TIGER OFFICER
PEOPLE SMUGGLER (Indonesian)
ASYLUM SEEKERS

ACT THREE

APAH, 80s
LILY, 20s
RADHA, 48
SIDDHARTHA, 20
ISMET
NIHINSA, 50s

HASA, 30s

RADHA, 27

PRIEST, 70s

THIRRU, 27

FRUIT SELLER (Tamil-speaking Sri Lankan, no English)

PETTAH SHOP OWNER (Tamil-speaking Sri Lankan)

OPERATOR (Singhalese-speaking Sri Lankan)

PETTAH POLICE COMMANDER

WELAWATTE SHOP OWNER (Tamil-speaking Sri Lankan, broken
English)

INSPECTOR GENERAL OF POLICE

MRS. KUMARASWAMY

RECEPTIONIST TO THE PRESIDENT

PRESIDENT

JANINI

MAYA

ARIF

KUNTHAVI

HOOLIGANS

VINSANDA, 80s

MESSENGER (Singhalese-speaking Sri Lankan, broken English)

DHAMAYANTHI, 50s

FUNERAL PROCESSION

SUNIL, 40s

FURNITURE MOVERS

HASA, 50s

ASYLUM SEEKERS

Ensemble to play COMMENTATORS, WEDDING GUESTS, ASYLUM
SEEKERS, HOOLIGANS, FUNERAL PROCESSION, FURNITURE
MOVERS

SETTING

The play takes place between 1956 and 2004.

Act One

The banks of the Georges River, Haigh Park, Liverpool; Sully Street, Coogee; Radha's apartment, Pendle Hill; Welikada Prison, Colombo; Siddhartha's and Ismet's neighbouring houses, Coogee; the front porch of Sunil's home, Milagiriya Avenue, Colombo.

Act Two

The front porch of the family home, Milagiriya Avenue, Colombo; Radha's apartment, Pendle Hill; the front porch of Sunil's home, Milagiriya Avenue, Colombo; a remote beach near Banda Aceh, Indonesia; the Indian Ocean.

Act Three

The front porch of the family home, Milagiriya Avenue, Colombo; Siddhartha's front yard, Coogee; Radha's apartment, Pendle Hill; various stores, offices and streets around Colombo; a train to Villawood; Villawood Detention Centre.

ACT ONE

SCENE ONE

Haigh Park, Western Sydney. 2004. The banks of the Georges River.

A Hindu PRIEST *sits on the ground. He chants in Sanskrit.*

SIDDHARTHA *sits beside him. He holds a small ornate urn. He wears jeans but is bare-chested. His shirt and shoes are on the ground nearby.*

RADHA *stands behind* SIDDHARTHA, *watching him closely. She is dressed in a saree and carries a tote bag.*

The PRIEST *chants, swiftly and precisely.* SIDDHARTHA *repeats each line of the chant. He struggles with the unfamiliar words, and, in his Australian accent, with their pronunciation. Occasionally the* PRIEST *repeats a phrase and* SIDDHARTHA *attempts it again. As he chants the* PRIEST *guides* SIDDHARTHA *through the actions and gestures of the ceremony: he ties long grass around his finger, pours rice from a plate into a bowl, blesses a small fire.*

The PRIEST *stops chanting and stands.* SIDDHARTHA *stands too: still holding the urn.*

PRIEST: குடும்பத்தில இருந்து யாராவது ஒரு ஆம்பிள்ள அவரோட கூடப் போக வேணும். (A male from the family should go in with him.)

RADHA: ஒருத்தரும் மிச்சமில்ல. (There is no-one left.)

> *Beat.*

PRIEST: [*looking at the urn*] உங்கள்ண்ட அம்மாவுக்குத் தெரிஞ்சவே யாராவது. (Someone who knew your mother.)

RADHA: ஐயர் நீங்கள் [போவீங்களா]? (Ayar. Would you?)

PRIEST: நாளைக்கு யாரையாவது [பிடிச்சுக்] கொண்டு வாங்கோ. மிச்சத்தை அதுக்குப் பிறகு செய்வம். (Find someone and bring them tomorrow. We'll finish the rites then.)

RADHA: எங்கட அம்மாவ உங்களுக்குத் தெரியும் … தெரிஞ்சவ ஒருத்தரும் இங்க இல்ல. (There is no-one. Please. You knew my mother.)

Beat.

PRIEST: [*sympathetic*] Okay. [*To* SIDDHARTHA, *in English*] Come. Together, together.

He walks into the river.

SIDDHARTHA: Do I follow?

RADHA: Into the river.

SIDDHARTHA: Are you serious?

RADHA: No questions.

SIDDHARTHA: I should have worn shorts.

RADHA: Jeans is bad enough. Your *ammamma* would be disgusted.

SIDDHARTHA: I'm not sure we should walk into the Georges River. It looks pretty green. This is probably illegal.

RADHA: Kunthavi Aunty did her mother's funeral rites here and said it was fine.

SIDDHARTHA: Oh if an aunty said so … Can I put my shirt back on?

RADHA: I don't think anyone cares about your stupid body that looks like a stick.

SIDDHARTHA: So can I?

RADHA: No. Go. *Go.*

SIDDHARTHA *follows the* PRIEST *into the shallows.*

The PRIEST *chants in Sanskrit, then:*

PRIEST: [*English, to* SIDDHARTHA] Okay okay, now, you.

The PRIEST *gestures to* SIDDHARTHA. SIDDHARTHA *looks to* RADHA, *confused.*

[*To* RADHA] அஸ்திய தண்ணீல கலக்க சொல்லுங்கோ. (He must release the ashes.)

RADHA: [*to* SIDDHARTHA] You must let the ashes go into the water.

SIDDHARTHA: Yes.

PRIEST: [*English*] Let go. Let go.

SIDDHARTHA *slowly empties the contents of the urn into the water.*

Without looking at SIDDHARTHA, *the* PRIEST *takes the urn and returns to the bank.*

RADHA: Come.

SIDDHARTHA: [*returning to the bank*] That's it?

RADHA: No questions! Yes.

SIDDHARTHA: That's it.

RADHA: That's it. Good boy. Why are you crying? I'm not crying.

SIDDHARTHA: [*crying*] I'm not crying.

RADHA: Now she can rest. Put your clothes back on. Here.

She takes a towel from her bag.

What, Siddhartha?

SIDDHARTHA: What?

RADHA: Don't think at me.

SIDDHARTHA: I don't understand anything that's—

RADHA: Your *ammamma* doted on you. Even when you left she didn't say anything—

SIDDHARTHA: Amma—

RADHA: She doted on you. Now she can rest. Now I have to do all the worrying about you.

SIDDHARTHA *puts his shirt back on.*

Will you move back home now?

SIDDHARTHA: Amma …

RADHA: You've been in Bondi for six months.

SIDDHARTHA: Coogee, Amma. Bondi's full of backpackers.

RADHA: What's wrong with Pendle Hill?

SIDDHARTHA: Coogee's closer to uni. I've told you this. I study better.

RADHA: What is media studies anyway?

SIDDHARTHA: Amma—I should go. I don't want to—I'll call you in a week or so. / And come over for dinner.

RADHA: Fine.

SIDDHARTHA: / We don't have to fight.

RADHA: / Off you go.

SIDDHARTHA: / I'm glad I came.

RADHA: Take the towel for the train. Don't wreck it. Wash it carefully in a delicate cycle and bring / it back.

SIDDHARTHA: Amma—

RADHA: Go. I want to talk to the priest.

Beat.

Left to right: Nadie Kammallaweera, Rarriwuy Hick, Shiv Palekar and Gandhi MacIntyre in the Belvoir/Co-Curious production. Photo: Brett Boardman.

SIDDHARTHA: I'll come over soon okay. [*To the* PRIEST] Thank you. Goodbye.

PRIEST: No goodbyes!

SIDDHARTHA *is confused.*

RADHA: In Tamil we don't say goodbye. Only, I will go and come back.

SIDDHARTHA: Okay. I will go and [*leaving, as The Terminator*] I'll be back!

He goes.

RADHA: Stupid boy.

She gives the PRIEST *two fifty-dollar notes.*

அவ என்னோட இருக்கிறத விட, தன்ர ஆக்களோட இருக்கிறதத் தான் விரும்புவா. (My mother will be happier with her ancestors than she was with me.)

PRIEST: *Chi.*

RADHA: She didn't raise me, *ayar.* My grandparents did. And Nihinsa—

PRIEST: Radha. [*He gestures to say 'enough'.*] She is home now.

Beat.

RADHA: Ayar. Twenty-one years ago I left Sri Lanka with my son in here [*touching her belly*] and my grandfather's ashes in a Tupperware container. Nine years ago my father's ashes were handed to me by this sweet woman named Shirley at Rookwood Crematorium. My accountant took them back to Sri Lanka in his suitcase and my father's ashes were scattered in the Kelani river. Today, his wife's ashes have been poured into the Georges River, and they are together again. No more violence. No more exile. No more waste. Ayar. My grandfather's ashes have been sitting under my bed for twenty-one years.

The PRIEST *looks at her.*

தெரியும் … அவர் நல்ல கோபத்தில இருப்பார். (I know. He'd be furious.)

The PRIEST *keeps looking at her.*

சண்ட முடியட்டும் எண்டு பாத்துக் கொண்டிருந்தனான் …

திரும்பப் போகலாம் எண்டு நினச்சன் … (Maybe I was waiting for the fighting to end. Before going back home again …)

PRIEST: Apah's ashes have been under your bed?

RADHA: In Pendle Hill. For twenty-one years. *Ayar* …

She takes a small Tupperware container from her bag.

Please.

Beat.

PRIEST: உங்கட மகன் தான் இத செய்யோணும். (Your son should do this.)

RADHA: அவன ஏன் கரச்சல் பண்ணிக் கொண்டு? அவனுக்கு ஒண்டும் விளங்கப் போறதுமில்ல. அவன் இப்ப ஒஸ்ரேலியாவில. கூஜியில இருக்கிறான் … Media studies படிக்கிறான். (Why bother the poor child? He doesn't understand all that. He's in Australia now. In Coogee. Studying media studies.) What does that mean? Studying studies?

PRIEST: மன்னிக்கோணும் ராதா … அப்பிடிச் செய்யேலாது. (Radha. I'm sorry, no.)

With his hands he gestures: I'm sorry, no.

RADHA: அப்பிடியெண்டா? (Then what?)

PRIEST: செய்யேக்க ஒழுங்கா செய்யோணும். சரியான நேரத்தில செய்யோணும். இப்ப இல்ல. (It must be done properly, at the right time. No.)

Again the PRIEST gestures: I'm sorry, no.

RADHA: சரியான நேரம் பிழையான நேரமாப் போச்சு. (The right time was the wrong time.)

PRIEST: சரியான நேரம் வரைக்கும் காத்திருக்கோணும். (You must wait for the right time again.) Apah was my friend. No.

Again the PRIEST gestures: I'm sorry, no. The sound of a car horn.

RADHA: ஐயர் … (Ayar …)

PRIEST: மருமகப் பொடியன் என்ன woolliesக்குக் கொண்டு போறான். அவன்ர அப்பர மாதிரி அவனுக்கும் அவசரம். (My nephew is taking me to Woolworths. He drives too fast. Like his father.)

Beat.

RADHA: சரி. (Okay.)

PRIEST: போயிட்டு வாறன். (Goodbye.)

RADHA: போயிட்டு வாங்கோ. (Goodbye.)

The PRIEST *begins to leave.*

[*Calling after him*] You should try the Aldi's in Bankstown. Their prices are much better.

The PRIEST *is gone.*

RADHA *puts the Tupperware back in her bag.*

நீங்களும் நானும் மட்டும் தான் இப்ப … தாத்தா. (Just you and me now, Grandfather.)

SCENE TWO

Sully Street, Coogee, 2004. Distant sound of party.

SIDDHARTHA *and* LILY *are walking away from the party to the park opposite. Both are drunk.* SIDDHARTHA *is struggling to roll a joint. He is wound up.*

SIDDHARTHA: See people think they're talking to each other but we don't really see each other—we see the image of what we are, not what we fucking actually are. Soon …

He takes out his Nokia 6630.

… we're gonna have phones that have tiny friggin' cameras and TVs in them and we're gonna become just—simulations performing for each other. What Baudrillard calls simulacrums. Can you hold my phone? [*He throws it to her.*] Thanks. It's like, the only way humans can handle living together is if we all live in our own virtual realities. Tiny, isolated, private universes. Thanks for dancing with me, by the way. You're an excellent dancer.

LILY: You're a brave dancer.

SIDDHARTHA: Thank you.

He puts the rolled joint in his jeans pocket and starts feeling for his lighter.

We're disconnected. Waiting for the wave to crash. I'm

paraphrasing now. John someone, uh—'We are waiting with the cruel, / experienced eye—

LILY: We're quoting now?

SIDDHARTHA: —cruel, experienced eye of a citizenry that has lost respect for its leadership in general but hasn't quite worked out what to / do about it—'[1]

LILY: Here's one for ya. 'We have successfully constructed political systems in which the power of the state is constrained. This success lies in recognising that power can only be controlled by power.'

SIDDHARTHA: Faaaaark. Who said that? Thomas Jefferson? / Lincoln?

LILY: / What? No!

SIDDHARTHA: Mao? Trotsky! Foucault!

LILY: Idiot. It's what they tell senators when they get inducted into the Australian Parliament.

SIDDHARTHA: Law. You're a law student.

LILY: Gold star to you, kiddo.

SIDDHARTHA: Can you guess what I'm studying?

LILY: Mate you're clearly an arts student.

SIDDHARTHA: Arts and media studies.

LILY: What even is that?

Siddhartha's phone starts ringing.

SIDDHARTHA: Why do people keep asking me that?!

LILY: Your phone's ringing.

SIDDHARTHA: It's alright. It's just Amma.

LILY: Who's that?

SIDDHARTHA: Amma. Means Mum.

LILY: Then answer it!

SIDDHARTHA: She's a Lankan mum! Shit's urgent all the time, y'know? She calls me at five a.m. to catch me at parties and make sure I'm alive and stuff.

LILY: Is that normal Sri Lankan mum behaviour, or—

SIDDHARTHA: Pretty normal, in my experience. But no definitely not. Even for a Lankan mum she's like fully over the top. Do you have a lighter?

LILY: I've got some Sri Lankan in me.

---

1 *The Collapse of Globalism*, John Ralston Saul

SIDDHARTHA: You do?!

LILY: This DNA scientist came up to our place and took swabs from inside our cheeks. Couple of months later they told us we've got Sri Lankan in us.

SIDDHARTHA: From when?

LILY: About four thousand years ago.

SIDDHARTHA: Faaaaaaaark!

LILY: Right?

SIDDHARTHA: So some Lankan fisherman or something made their way to Australia four thousand years ago?

LILY: Maybe. My aunties reckon they were traders.

SIDDHARTHA: That's three thousand eight hundred years before the English came.

LILY: Yep …

SIDDHARTHA: Wow. Prior claim, white guys.

LILY: What?

SIDDHARTHA: Shit sorry / I'm a moron. Respect—

LILY: Tell me about your mum.

SIDDHARTHA: [*laughing, defensively*] What?

LILY: Ahah! Tell me about your mum.

SIDDHARTHA: Why?

LILY: Do it, Mister Eyelashes.

SIDDHARTHA: Excuse me?

LILY: Tell me about your mum!

SIDDHARTHA: [*laughing*] I don't know. She's my mum. We fight. I moved out of home. She stopped talking to me. I don't know.

LILY: Why'd you move out of home?

SIDDHARTHA: Cause we fight all the time.

LILY: Why do you fight?

SIDDHARTHA: [*laughing*] How would I know? I fight with my amma. She fought with her amma. That's what we do.

LILY: How come she's calling you if she stopped talking to you?

SIDDHARTHA: Because my ammamma got sick—

LILY: Ammamma?

SIDDHARTHA: My mum's mum.

LILY: Amma's amma.

SIDDHARTHA: That's it.

LILY: Then what happened?

SIDDHARTHA: Why do you want to know?!

LILY: Come on, Eyelashes. Why did your amma fight with her amma?

SIDDHARTHA: I don't know.

LILY: Ask your ammamma.

SIDDHARTHA: She died. A few days ago.

LILY: I'm sorry.

SIDDHARTHA: No that's okay. It was time. That sounds a bit—I loved her, I really loved my ammamma. Her name was Dhamayanthi. She always wore blue. She spoilt me. She never told me anything. 'Cept just before she died she leans over to me and whispers, 'You were the only good thing that came out of your parents' marriage.' She told me that.

LILY: What about your dad?

SIDDHARTHA: Ha! No dad. He died. Also.

LILY: I'm sorry.

SIDDHARTHA: It's okay. It was before I was born.

LILY: Was he Sri Lankan?

SIDDHARTHA: I think so. His name was Thirru Sivakumar. Which I only know 'cos Amma had to give me my birth certificate when I got a passport.

LILY: So where were you born?

SIDDHARTHA: Here. Liverpool Hospital. 1983. Amma came to Australia when she was pregnant with me. And that's it, okay? That's all I know!

LILY: Why don't you ask your mum—

SIDDHARTHA: You ask my mum!

LILY: I will.

SIDDHARTHA: I fucking won't. She's a black hole. If I get too close I'll be— It's cold. Aren't you cold?

LILY: So you're Tamil? You're not— what's the other—

SIDDHARTHA: Singhalese. Nah, we're Tamil. We're the minority. But my name's Sinhalese. And I don't speak Tamil, and I've never been to Sri Lanka. Here I am with too much English, a Sinhala name, no Tamil and some very bad Spanish. I'm a terrible Sri Lankan. Muy terriblé!

LILY: [*warmly*] Idiot.

SIDDHARTHA: Today was Ammamma's funeral. I chanted Sanskrit and poured her ashes into the Georges River. I thought before she died she might tell me, you know.

> *Pause. He rubs his arms, still shivering a little.*

That DNA scientist guy. Came up to 'our place' you said. Our place. Where's that?

LILY: Up North. Yolngu people.

SIDDHARTHA: Arnhem Land. Saltwater people.

LILY: Yeah. [*Beat*] My family are all in Yirrkala.

SIDDHARTHA: Yirrkala. Sounds like Tamil. Tell me about Yirrkala.

LILY: Oh you know. Red dirt. Deserted beaches.

SIDDHARTHA: C'mon.

LILY: Crocs. Sharks—

SIDDHARTHA: Yeah yeah, lots of animals that'll kill ya and skies full of stars. I've seen the ads. Tell me about your home.

> LILY *sizes him up.*

LILY: My *Namala*—that's what we call our birth mums—she paints the stars.

SIDDHARTHA: Uh huh.

LILY: She painted me this story once. About the Milky Way. She drew this … massive body of water in the sky.

> LILY *draws a circle in the air above them.*

It's where we live for eternity. We're all these tiny little fish that just swim up in there.

> LILY *fills the circle with lots of small crosses.*

SIDDHARTHA: Huh.

LILY: And when the time comes to go down to earth, we get to pick who our parents are. You choose your amma, you know?

SIDDHARTHA: Woah.

LILY: So we come down from the Milky Way and swim to our chosen parents. And we live our lives down here, all this … stuff … but at the end we go back up there—in our *Larrpan*, this beautiful canoe—to *Baralku*, our island in the sky.

SIDDHARTHA: Back up there—to the Milky Way?

LILY: Yeah.

SIDDHARTHA: Huh.

LILY: What?

SIDDHARTHA: Well … You know how the stars and planets and stuff are all moving, right? Here.

He stands up. Pauses.

Even like this— [*He becomes completely still.*] We're floating in space right now. We're moving. We're *always* moving. Right?

LILY: Yeah …

SIDDHARTHA: According to Ammamma, that mass of stars and galaxies is a dolphin in the sky. And the Milky Way is its belly. And all that movement? The flow of the stars? Ammamma called it the Ganges of the sky.

LILY: So we have *Baralku*. And you have the Ganges.

SIDDHARTHA: Water and water, Ammamma always used to say. Water and water. Down here, up there— [*He leans in and touches her belly*] and in here too. It's all one thing, you know?

She nods.

They kiss.

LILY: Sun's coming up.

SIDDHARTHA: Um. I don't even know your name.

LILY: I'm Lily. And my Yolngu name is Yumalil.

SIDDHARTHA: Hi Yumalil. [*Beat*] I'm Siddhartha.

LILY: Sid—what—now?

SIDDHARTHA: Siddhartha. It was Buddha's name before he became, well, Buddha.

LILY: Hi Siddhartha.

Beat.

SIDDHARTHA: What's the date today, Lily?

LILY: It's the ninth of March.

He looks at the phone, then her.

SIDDHARTHA: Five a.m. on the ninth of March, 2004.

LILY: Yep.

SIDDHARTHA: Five a.m. On the ninth of March. 2004.

SCENE THREE

Radha's apartment in Pendle Hill.

An ornate wooden Sri Lankan armchair. The Tupperware container with Apah's ashes sits on the chair.

RADHA *stuffs clothes and household items into large garbage bags: sarees, a cricket bat, medical items, etc. With her shoulder she holds a cordless phone to her ear.*

RADHA: I don't know, I rang the number on the Holroyd Council website and pressed three or nine and held and pressed five for—

    The intercom buzzes.

—hard rubbish, half an hour later I got through to you. [*Listening*] Hard rubbish collection, obviously. [*Listening*] Hard. Rubbish. [*Listening*] I don't want to make a noise complaint.

    The intercom buzzes.

Yes yes yes, wait wait wait, one moment, please. [*She answers the intercom*] Hold, please. [*Back to the phone*] No not you. [*Listening*] *Moorooha!* Look mister I don't know, I followed the prompts— [*Listening*] Well if you want a noise complaint you just keeping asking me what I'm ringing for. [*Listening*] Hard rubbish— May I put an idea—

    The intercom buzzes three times.

—to you. Pardon me. [*Intercom*] One moment, please. [*Telephone*] At my workplace everybody has a little piece of laminated paper with all the telephone extensions. Do you— [*Listening*] Then perhaps—

    The intercom buzzes several times insistently.

—you could— One moment, please. [*She goes to the balcony*] You on my intercom, what do you want?

ISMET: [*offstage, thick Turkish accent*] Air conditioner!

RADHA: Okay don't shout at me! [*Telephone*] Yes mister, I hope this is being recorded for coaching and training purposes because this is not a successful conversation.

ISMET: [*offstage*] Hello!

RADHA: [*to* ISMET] What do you want? [*Telephone*] No, I don't know what 'zone' I'm in, I'm in Pendle Hill, you should tell me. Yes, I'll hold.

ISMET: [*offstage*] Mrs Radha Sivakumar?

RADHA: Yes!

ISMET: [*offstage*] Your son rang me to install an air conditioner.

RADHA: Yes!

ISMET: [*offstage*] Yes?

RADHA: Yes come up already! First floor.

She buzzes him in.

ISMET: [*offstage*] Yes!

RADHA: Okay! [*Telephone*] Hello? [*Listening*] I can't wait that long—

The intercom buzzes.

[*Intercom*] I told you come up!

FUNDRAISER: [*intercom*] வணக்கம் அம்மா … எப்படி இருக்கிறீங்கள்? சித்தார்த்தா சிவக்குமார் இருக்கிறாரே? (Madam! How are you? Is Siddhartha Sivakumar there?)

Beat.

RADHA: Are you also the air conditioner man?

FUNDRAISER: [*intercom*] Madam—

The doorbell rings.

RADHA: [*intercom*] Wait one moment. [*Opens the door to* ISMET] Do you have a Tamil man with you?

ISMET: What?

RADHA: [*intercom*] Who are you? Just one moment. [*Telephone*] Yes I'm still here. [*Listening*] Sir, my capacity to hold will astonish you. [*Listening*] That's a yes. [*To* ISMET] Yes?

ISMET: I will now measure your wall.

RADHA: [*pointing*] That one. [*Intercom*] Please, who are you?

FUNDRAISER: [*now in the doorway behind her*] வணக்கம் … மிஸ்ஸிஸ் சிவக்குமார்? (Hello. Mrs Sivakumar?)

RADHA: கடவுளே … (Kadavallay!) How did you get up here?

FUNDRAISER: மன்னிக்கோணும் … வெளிக்கதவுதிறந்திருந்தது. (Sorry madam, the security door was open.)

ISMET: My fault.

RADHA: [*to* FUNDRAISER] கதவு திறந்திருந்தா ... உள்ள வாறதே? (So you just wander in?) [*To* ISMET] Where are you going?

ISMET: To get my tools.

He goes.

RADHA: [*calling after him*] Where is my air conditioner? [*Telephone*] Hello? [*Nothing. To* FUNDRAISER] Who are you?

FUNDRAISER: சித்தார்த்தா சிவக்குமார் இருக்கிறாரே? (Is Siddhartha Sivakumar here, madam?)

RADHA: No.

FUNDRAISER: இல்லையே (No?)

Beat.

[*Giving her a leaflet*] எங்கட பொடியங்கள் செய்யிற நல்ல வேலைகளைப் பாருங்கோ. இது, முல்லத் தீவில ஒரு பள்ளிக்கூடம் நடத்திறாங்கள். கிளிநொச்சியில சனத்துக்கு சாப்பாடு போடுறாங்கள். (Please. See the fantastic work the boys have been doing. Here is the school in Mullaitivu. Here they are giving food to the families in Kilinochchi.)

RADHA: What do you want?

FUNDRAISER: நல்ல வடிவா பள்ளிக்கூடம் நடத்திறதப் பாருங்கோ ... இதெல்லாம், எங்கட ஆக்கள் ஒஸ்ரேலியா, கனடா, லண்டன், ஃப்ரான்ஸ் இல இருந்து அனுப்பிற காச வைச்சு நடக்குது. (See what a top shelf school it is. We do all this with funds from Tamil families in Australia, Canada, the UK, France—)

RADHA: You want money? From me?

FUNDRAISER: தொகையப் பத்தி கவலை இல்லை. நீங்கள் சின்னதா குடுத்தா என்ன பெரிசாக் குடுத்தா என்ன வாங்குவம். (If you're offering, every amount big or small—)

RADHA: These are the Tigers.

FUNDRAISER: Yes.

RADHA: Why would I do that?

Beat.

FUNDRAISER: அம்மா. ... நாப்பது வருஷமா இந்த உலகமே எங்கள ஏறெடுத்தும் பாக்கேல்ல. இப்ப, விடுதலைப் புலிகளால நாங்கள்

யார், எங்களுக்கு என்ன நடக்குதெண்டு உலகத்துக்குத் தெரியுது. இந்த சந்தர்ப்பத்த நாங்கள் விடக்கூடாது. தமிழீழம் எங்களுக்கு இப்ப கிடைக்க வேண்டுமெண்டா நாங்கள் ஒற்றுமையா நடக்க வேண்டிய அலுவல பாக்க வேணும். உங்கட தாத்தா ஒரு பெரியா ஆள் ... எங்களுக்கெல்லாம் அப்பா மாதிரி. (Madam, for forty years the world ignored us. Now, because of the Tigers, we are front page news. We are Prime Time! We have to seize this opportunity. We must unite and do whatever is necessary to create a homeland of Tamil Eelam. Your grandfather is a hero of our cause. Your Apah is like a father to all of us.)

She hangs up the phone.

RADHA: This morning my priest told me about a fruit seller in Jaffna. He'd just been married, and not long after the wedding, completely by mistake, he delivered some mangoes to one of the Sri Lankan army houses. He was accused by the Tigers of being an informant. He was shot on his bicycle, dragged along Point Pedro Rd, and strung up on the tree near Lingan Ice Cream House. Was that 'necessary'? His new wife was ordered to wear the white saree of a widow. அது (தேவைதானா) தேவதானா? (Was that 'necessary'?)

FUNDRAISER: Madam—

RADHA *points to the Tupperware container on the chair.*

RADHA: இது என்ர அப்பா. ... விடுதலை புலிகளைப்பற்றி சொல்ற அதே வாயால, அவரைப் பத்தி கதைக்க வேண்டாம். உங்கட ஆக்களுக்குப் போய்ச் சொல்லும், இனி நான் தான் அவருக்காவண்டி கதைப்பன் எண்டு. கேட்டுதே. நீங்கள் செய்யிற வேலைக்கு, கடவுளே மன்னிக்க மாட்டார். (That is my grandfather. You do not mention him ever again in the same breath as the Tigers. Tell that to your organisation. Tell them I speak for him now. Do you hear?)

She hands back the leaflet.

(Even the gods won't forgive you for what you are doing.)

Beat.

FUNDRAISER: The gods have never had to suffer like our people have had to suffer, madam. [*Still very polite*] சரி அம்மா ... நான்

சந்திக்க வந்தது, உங்கட மகன் சித்தார்த்தா. (You know, the person I came to speak to is your son. Siddhartha Sivakumar.)

RADHA: I beg your pardon?

FUNDRAISER: உங்கட மகன் ஒரு நாளும் நாட்டுக்குப் போனதில்ல மிஸ்ஸிஸ் சிவக்குமார். அவரை நாட்டுக்கு நீங்க அனுப்ப வேணும். உங்கட மகனைப் போல விவேகமான ஆக்கள் இணைஞ்சாத்தான், தமிழ்ப் போராட்டம் வெல்லும். (He has never been to his homeland, Mrs Sivakumar. You should send your son to Sri Lanka. The Tamil struggle will never be won without bright young men like Siddhartha—)

RADHA: Get out.

FUNDRAISER: Madam—

RADHA: Get out of here and don't come back.

FUNDRAISER: I think you know what happens to people who disagree with us—

RADHA: Get out. Out. Out.

FUNDRAISER: Okay, okay, relax, relax. What do they say here? No worries. No worries.

He goes and she closes the door behind him.

Shaken, she sits in the armchair and closes her eyes.

RADHA: One equals zero point nine nine nine nine nine nine—

The doorbell rings.

She snatches up the cricket bat and opens the door.

Murderer. Liar. You touch my son—

ISMET: [*carrying boxes*] Isa Meryem ve-Yusuf! It is just the poor air conditioner man.

Beat.

RADHA: Yes. Come.

ISMET: My doctor says I have blocked arteries—

RADHA: I'm very sorry—

ISMET: Do you want to give me a heart attack?

RADHA: No no. Sorry. Come. Please. Thank you. No. Wait. This is not my air conditioner.

ISMET: Ah. No. But I would not be doing my job if I did not—

RADHA: The KC10WR is what I asked for.

ISMET: Maybe in a smaller room than this one—

RADHA: Its mean air velocity at three metres per second equals a volumetric flow that is more than / capable of—

ISMET: That's just numbers.

RADHA: I worked this out—five cubic metres per minute—

ISMET: I know from experience. Maybe I should talk to your husband—

RADHA: Do you see a husband?

ISMET: … No.

RADHA: Is there something that makes you think it's not possible that I might be a trained mathematician?

ISMET: … Yes. No. I don't—

RADHA: At Cambridge University there is a mathematics scholarship in my maiden name.

ISMET: Well—

RADHA: The Mannikavasar Scholarship for Mathematical Excellence.

ISMET: Very good.

RADHA: Do not try to up-sell me, Mister Air Conditioner.

ISMET: Okay, okay! You win! The Kelvinator KC10WR goes—

RADHA: There.

ISMET: Exactly where I would put it myself.

RADHA: So go get it.

ISMET: I will. In a moment. Of course.

He re-measures the wall and sets to work preparing to cut a hole in the wall.

RADHA: Good. [*Beat.*] I expect a discount, with all the advice I have given you already. Do you want a tea or coffee?

ISMET: Coffee. Please.

RADHA: You live next door to my son?

ISMET: He saw my van in the driveway. 'Ismet Air-flows'. I have a big sign.

RADHA: If you see my son tell him I have sent his cricket gear to the rubbish.

ISMET: Yes ma'am.

RADHA: Does he have parties?

ISMET: … I haven't heard any parties.

Beat.

RADHA: The mathematics scholarship is named after my grandfather, not me. A small lie. I apologise. Love cake?

ISMET: Sorry?

RADHA: I made a love cake, do you want a piece?

ISMET: Is the cake as sweet as you?

RADHA: Am I sweet?

ISMET: Understood. Love cake would be lovely.

RADHA: I dislike air conditioners. Where I grew up we had high ceilings, spinning fans, open spaces. A chair was placed specifically to catch a certain breeze. Here, everything is divided. We must force air into a place.

ISMET: Where did you grow up?

RADHA: Continue your job, mister.

ISMET: My *job* is to pay my rent and my alimony. This [*pointing to the air conditioner*] allows me to do that. And this [*the cake*] is delicious. Thank you, ah …

RADHA: Yes?

ISMET: I am Ismet.

RADHA: Ismet Air-flows. [*Beat*] Radha.

ISMET: Radha. Beautiful. 'Mrs' Sivakumar, you see—it is the name of a woman with a husband. I didn't mean to intrude. Well, maybe I did. But not to offend.

RADHA: It's okay.

ISMET: *My* wife left me—I am not ashamed to say it—for a richer man, back home in Lebanon. My son went with her.

He continues working.

My son, do I see him? No. Can I talk to him? No. He tells me, Dad, don't call on the phone! It's too expensive! Call on the computer. A telephone on a computer? I say. You want your father to telephone you on a computer? Me who used to run beside you chasing pigeons and picking the gumnuts out of the soles of your dirty feet to stop you from crying? I should call you on a computer? People change. Did your husband change?

RADHA: No.

ISMET: You left him? He left you?

RADHA: No.

> *Beat.*

ISMET: I am a very good person to talk to, Radha. I am! I have had three countries, two children, two wives and four dogs. I have spent a lot of time listening to all of them. None of them have ever listened to me but that is beside the point.

RADHA: My husband is dead.

> *Beat.*

ISMET: I'm sorry.

RADHA: The government in Sri Lanka took him and killed him.

ISMET: Very sorry.

> *Beat.*

RADHA: Well. There it is. It was twenty-one years ago, I should talk about it with someone. Why not the air conditioner man?

ISMET: Why not?

> *Pause.*

That man who was here—?

RADHA: Rubbish. Fundraising for violence. Nothing to do with me.

ISMET: I see.

RADHA: You said *two* wives?

> *She sits in the chair and watches him.*

ISMET: The first one was Palestinian. In Lebanon. The second, Australian. You know, a blonde Australian.

RADHA: And they both left you?

ISMET: What can I say? I am an optimist. [*Beat*] You know, my ancestors were generals in the Ottoman Empire. You should try a Turkish man. We win our wars.

RADHA: Malta.

ISMET: Excuse me?

RADHA: Malta, an island nation smaller even than Sri Lanka, was able to ward off the mighty Turkish empire at its height.

> *Beat.*

ISMET: You are a remarkable woman.

She laughs.

Well, if not a Turkish man—how about a [*he walks over to her with a small bag*] Turkish delight?

RADHA: No thank you.

ISMET: This is the good stuff. I'll leave it here. You can have it later.

RADHA: Install my air conditioner, Mister Air-flows.

He smiles and returns to work.

She sits back in the chair.

She looks at Apah's ashes.

She looks back at Ismet.

You should talk to my son about your computer telephone.

He laughs and turns to look at her.

ISMET: Maybe I will.

RADHA: Go on then.

He laughs again and returns to work.

ISMET: Sri Lanka. It is like a paradise, people tell me.

RADHA: Yes. It is. But not for all.

ISMET: Do you go back there?

RADHA *gets up to clear away the tea.*

RADHA: No. Look how much Australia has given to us. I focus on here now.

She eats the Turkish Delight.

Now put a hole in my wall, Ismet. Get me some air-flows in here!

SCENE FOUR

Wellikade Prison, Colombo, 2004.

A man, THIRRU, *walks around the perimeter of his tiny cell.*

His careful steps have the quality of a practiced action or ritual. He has a battered old copy of a book. He whispers sections of the book to himself, checking his memory as he goes.

Outside the cell, a jailor has a small transistor radio which broadcasts

Sinhalese commentary from the 2004 Australia-Sri Lanka test match in Kandy.

The JAILOR speaks to the audience in Sinhala. Cricketing and scientific terms are in English.

JAILOR: යාලුවෝ මගෙන් අහනවා 'මොකද උඹ වැඩියෙන්ම මුරලිට ආස? උඹ දෙමළෙක්නෙ ... අපි සිංහලනේ!' 'උඹ නොහිටින්න අපේ ටීම් එක නන්නත්තාරයි!' ....මං කෙළින්ම කියනවා. (My friends ask me why I like Murali the most when he is a Tamil, and we are all Singhalese. Obviously, I say, our team would be buggered without him.)

96දි ඔස්ට්‍රේලියාවේ ඩැරල් හෙයා කියන අම්පයර් ඉන්නේ ... මිනිහා දිගටම මුරලිට නෝ බෝල් දුන්නා, මුරලි බෝලෙ දාද්දි චක් කරනවා කියලා. හරි, කමක් නෑ කියමු. එක අම්පයර් කෙනෙක් විතරයිනේ. හැබැයි ඒකෙන් පස්සේ, මුරලි බෝලෙ දාන හැම්පාරම ප්‍රේක්ෂකාගාරේ හිටපු ඔස්ට්‍රේලියන් ජාතිකයෝ කෑගහන්න ගත්තා 'නෝ බෝල් කියලා!හරි,ඒකත් කමක් නෑ කියමු.ඒඑකමිනිස්සුකට්ටියක් විතරයිනේ. ඔන්න ඊළඟට ඔස්ට්‍රේලියාවේ අගමැති ජෝන් හවර්ඩ් ... මිනිහත් කියන්න ගත්තා මුරලි හොරට බෝලෙ දානවා කියලා! තත්වෙ ඔන්න ඔහොම තියෙද්දි ... බෲස් එලියට් කියලා විශ්වවිද්‍යාල ආචාර්යවරයෙක් කැමරා 12ක් දාලා, ත්‍රිමාන තාක්ෂණය පාවිච්චි කරලා පරීක්ෂා කරලා, හෙන ගේමක් දීලා ලෝකෙටම ඔප්පු කළා, මුරලිගෙ අවුලක් නෑ චක් කරන්නේ නැහැ කියලා. ඒ ආචාර්යවරයට නොපෙනුන මොනවහරි දෙයක්දිවැසින්. චත් පෙනුනද දන්නේ නෑ අර අගමැතියට. (Back in 1996, Australian Umpire Darrel Hare no-balled Murali many times for 'chucking'. Fine. That was just one umpire. After that Australian crowds would scream out 'no ball' whenever Murali was bowling. Fine. That was just some people. Then the Australian prime minister, John Howard, said Murali was chucking the ball too! A professor Bruce Elliott from a university used twelve cameras and 3D technology to test Murali, and said that he definitely wasn't chucking. What does the prime minister know that the professor doesn't?)

දැන් මුරලි ඔස්ට්‍රේලියාවේ සංචාරය කරන්නෑ එයා කියන්නේ අම්පයර්ට සමාව දෙන්න පුළුවන්,

ප්‍රේක්ෂකයන්ටත් සමාව දෙන්න පුළුවන්, හැබැයි ජෝන් හවඩ්ට සමාව දෙන්න බෑ කියලයි. (Now Murali refuses to tour to Australia. He says he can forgive the umpire, he can forgive the crowds, but he can't forgive John Howard.)

Beat.

2001දී මගේ අම්මයි තාත්තයි ආවා රණවිරු සමරුවකට. එදා ඒ සෙනග අතර ඉඳලා දෙමල කොටියෙක්, බැඳගෙන හිටපු බෝම්බේ පුපුරවාගන්නා. සිසිකඩ විසිරිලා තිබිච්ච අම්මගෙයි තාත්තගෙයි කොටස් ටික එකතු කරගන්න, එතන හිටපු පොලිස් රාළහාමි කෙනෙක් මට උදවු වුණා ... නැත්තන් මට ඒ දෙන්නව අඳුරගන්නවත් බැහැ (In 2001, my parents were at a service commemorating our army war heroes. A Tamil Tiger blew himself up in the middle of it. I couldn't properly identify my mother and father until a policeman helped me re-connect some of their body parts.)

අර මිනිහට වද දුන්නු හැම පාරම මම හිතුවේ ඒ දෙන්නා ගැන. ඒ පරයා මෙලෝ තොරතුරක් දුන්නෑ අපිට. සමහරවිට උ මොකුත් දන්නේ නැතුවත් ඇති. සමහරවිට උ නිකමෙක් වෙන්න ඇති. ඒත්, උට වේදනාවක් දැනෙන හැම වතාවෙම මට මොකද්දෝ පහසුවක් දැනුනා. (Every time I tortured that man [*he gestures to Thirru*] I thought of my parents. The bastard never gave us any information. Probably he doesn't know anything. Probably he is nobody in particular. Still I felt a little bit better every time he felt a little bit worse.)

The JAILOR *puts the radio down and walks up to* THIRRU. *He drags him to his feet, pushes him out of the cell and gives him an NGO-branded package of basic essentials.*

THIRRU: [*Tamil*] I don't understand.

JAILOR: No Tamil. Sinhala only.

THIRRU: මට තේරෙන්නේ නෑ (I don't understand.)

The JAILOR *looks through the package and takes most of it. Gives the rest to* THIRRU.

JAILOR: Someone has released you. Go!

In the cricket commentary, Muralitharan gets a wicket for Sri Lanka. THIRRU *listens:*

COMMENTARY: ඔව් ... මුරලිදරන් ඔහුගේ 500වැනි කඩුල්ල ලබාගන්නවා! කණ්ඩායමේ අනෙක් ක්‍රීඩකයන් උණුසුම් සුහැපැතුම් සමඟ ඔහුව වැලඳගන්නවා ... (And that's Muralitharan's five hundredth wicket! Look at the love from his team mates!)

JAILOR: කම්-ඔන් මචං! (Good one *machaan*!)

The JAILOR's focus returns to the cricket. With a slight wobble of the head, he indicates the man is free to go. As the man exits:

THIRRU: අවුරුද්ද? (What year is it?)

JAILOR: දෙදාස් හතර. (2004.)

THIRRU: Twenty-one years …

Confused and speechless, he takes his battered old book and exits.

COMMENTARY: ශේන් වොන් රැස් කර ඇති කඩුළු සංඛ්‍යාව පන්සිය එකයි.. ... මේ ටෙස්ට් තරඟයේදී ඔහුගේ වාර්තාව අභිබවා යන්නට මුරලිට හැකි වේද? (Shane Warne is on five hundred and one—can Murali overtake him within this test match, do you think?)

JAILOR: මුරලි කියන්නේ 'වෙනස්කම් නැති අපේ ක්‍රිකට් කණ්ඩායම දිහා බලලා, අපේ දෙකඩ වෙච්ච රට, ඉගෙනගන්න ඕනේ' කියලා. 'පහුගිය ප්‍රශ්න අමතක කරලා සමාව දෙන්න ඕනේ' කියලා. ඒත් මට බැහැ අමතක කරන්න. මං ලෑස්ති නෑ සමාව දෙන්න. මුරලි, ජෝන් හවඩ්ට, සමාව දෙන්නැහැනේ ... ඒ වගේ. (Murali says 'Our divided country should learn from our cricket team—no differences.' That we should 'forget our past troubles and forgive'. But I can't forget. And I won't forgive. Just like Murali won't forgive John Howard.)

SCENE FIVE

SIDDHARTHA *is on the front porch. He's playing solitaire and drinking a beer. The commentary repeats itself from the previous scene, this time in English.*

COMMENTARY: And Murali gets another wicket! Now he's even with Shane Warne …

SIDDHARTHA: Ooooooh.

ISMET: [*offstage*] Ary be hal computer, ary be emik! (Fuck this computer, fuck its mum.)

ISMET *enters.*

The world is shit! You.

SIDDHARTHA: Hello Ismet.

ISMET: Okay hello, polite, yes. Hello neighbour. Come with me.

SIDDHARTHA: I beg your pardon—

ISMET: I am trying to use Skippy to call my son in Turkey.

SIDDHARTHA: Skippy?

ISMET: Eh?

SIDDHARTHA: What is Skippy?

ISMET: How am I supposed to know? This is what your mother told me you would tell me. Come.

SIDDHARTHA: Ah so you met my—

ISMET: I want to use the phone. He says, no we don't pay for phone calls anymore. We use this Skippy.

SIDDHARTHA: Oh, Skype! It's Skype. Not Skippy.

ISMET: Doesn't matter. This boy, he wants to save two dollars on a phone call but he buys his kids stupid expensive presents they don't need. What is wrong with your generation, boy?

SIDDHARTHA: That sounds like something my mum would say.

ISMET: She is a good woman.

SIDDHARTHA: Did she tell how to do your job—

ISMET: Boy. Focus. I can't get my motherfucker computer to turn on. I don't have this Skippy program. My son is waiting for me to talk. Do you know these things? Will you help me?

Beat.

SIDDHARTHA: I'm waiting for someone.

ISMET: Son. I don't say this often. I need some help.

Beat.

SIDDHARTHA: Hold on.

SIDDHARTHA *writes a message on a small piece of paper.*

RADHA *enters her apartment. She sits in the chair, leans back and turns on the air conditioner.*

SIDDHARTHA *finishes writing.*

ISMET: Very good. Come!

SIDDHARTHA *and* ISMET *enter Ismet's study and* ISMET *points to the computer.*

There. Fix it.

SIDDHARTHA *checks the computer cables. He climbs under Ismet's table.*

My son says God is not real. He doesn't go to the mosque with his mother anymore. How can one be so arrogant as to not believe in God? Here we stick to it; over there, they have moved on. Here, I still have my chair that I made with my grandfather.

ISMET *hits the computer table hard.* SIDDHARTHA *gets a shock.*

Four generations old.

SIDDHARTHA: [*pressing the on button on the computer*] Wow. You made a chair?

ISMET: I made a chair. Still strong.

He hits the table again. SIDDHARTHA *jumps. The computer makes its 'on' sound.*

How did you do that? I have been trying to make that work for days!

SIDDHARTHA: A couple of cables were round the wrong way.

ISMET: Ibn al sharmouta. (Son of a whore.)

SIDDHARTHA: I need your son's Skype name …

ISMET *stares at him.*

Of course. That's okay, we'll find him, I just need his name, address— And I'll need to make you a Skype name too. Ismet, yeah?

ISMET *gives* SIDDHARTHA *a piece of paper with the details.*

RADHA *picks up the Turkish Delight.*

ISMET: Yes. And what was your name again, boy?

SIDDHARTHA: I'm Sid.

ISMET: You're Sri Lankan and you're called Sid? Sid is the brother of my blonde Australian second ex-wife. How can you be called Sid?

SIDDHARTHA: I'm not Sri Lankan, I'm Australian. My mum is Sri Lankan. And Sid is short for Siddhartha.

ISMET: What?

SIDDHARTHA: Siddhartha. It was Buddha's—

ISMET *stares at him.*

Oh forget it. [*He returns to the computer.*] We're almost there …

ISMET *starts typing on his phone.*

LILY *enters and reads Siddhartha's message.*

What are you doing?

ISMET: I'll tell you in a moment. Keep going.

SIDDHARTHA: I'm creating a user name called 'ISMETSKIPPY'. Awesome! It's available. You cool with that?

ISMET *grunts and continues typing on his phone.*

Okay then. And … done!

The Skype call starts ringing.

ISMET: Boy—

SIDDHARTHA: That's calling now.

ISMET: Can I ask you a question?

SIDDHARTHA: Sure but your Skype call's ringing.

ISMET: I am thinking maybe I will ask your mother out for dinner. What do you think?

SIDDHARTHA: Sorry? You—

ISMET: I'm going to send her a 'text', to ask her.

RADHA *puts the Turkish Delight in her mouth.*

LILY *picks up Siddhartha's beer and has a sip.*

SIDDHARTHA: Um …

ISMET: [*as in, couldn't hurt*] Why not?

SIDDHARTHA: You're going to what?

The Skype call stops ringing.

ISMET'S SON: Hello? Hello? Dad?

SIDDHARTHA: Are you seriously going to text my mum?

ISMET'S SON: Who's that?

ISMET: [*to* SIDDHARTHA] Sssssh. Ah— Hello?

ISMET'S SON: Dad? Where the hell have you been? I've been waiting for hours!

ISMET: [*turning to* SIDDHARTHA] Thank you.

ISMET'S SON: Dad?

ISMET: Wa'if yaa ibny, wa'if. (Wait son, wait.)

> ISMET *waves to* SIDDHARTHA *to go.*

SIDDHARTHA: I don't know what to say.

ISMET: Go home. The girl is waiting.

SIDDHARTHA: I'm not sure you—

ISMET: [*presses send*] There. I did it. I just asked your mother out for dinner!

> *Radha's phone beeps a message. Her mouth is full of Turkish Delight.*

> ISMET *turns and talks to his son in Arabic.*

> SIDDHARTHA *stands watching for a moment, then leaves in a hurry.*

> RADHA *looks at the message ... and laughs. The Turkish Delight erupts from her mouth. She puts her phone down.*

RADHA: The optimist! [*She laughs.*] Oh dear. Oh no. [*She laughs.*] Oh dear. Oh no.

> *Big cheers in the cricket commentary.*

> RADHA *gets a bottle of wine and a glass.*

Ridiculous.

> SIDDHARTHA *finds* LILY *on his porch.*

SIDDHARTHA: Hello.

LILY: Hi.

> *Pause.*

SIDDHARTHA: Hello.

LILY: Yeah, hi.

SIDDHARTHA: Yeah.

RADHA: Ridiculous.

LILY: ... You right?

SIDDHARTHA: Sorry I was just next door. Can I ... doesn't matter.

RADHA *laughs and wipes her eyes.*

RADHA: *Mooroha, Ganesha, Shiva …*
LILY: You talk a lot less during the daytime.
SIDDHARTHA: [*suddenly*] Can I take you to dinner tonight?

RADHA *pours a glass of wine.*

LILY: Yeah okay.
SIDDHARTHA: Okay. What time? Now? Or—
LILY: It's a bit early.
SIDDHARTHA: It is.
LILY: But yes, you can.
SIDDHARTHA: Good. Great. Great.

RADHA *drinks the whole glass of wine.*

LILY: Is that a full deck of cards?
SIDDHARTHA: Yeah.

LILY *sits down and shuffles expertly.*

RADHA *goes to her phone.*

LILY: I'll play you a game of rummy. Real money.
SIDDHARTHA: You're on. My ammamma taught me.
LILY: You should know my aunties taught me so just be prepared for me to kick your arse, and then you can take me to Iron Chef in Cabra. Cut the deck.

They begin to play.

Commentary continues through the radio.

RADHA *pours another glass of wine.*

ISMET *and his son talk away in a mixture of English and Arabic.*

SIDDHARTHA *opens another beer.*

RADHA *begins to write a reply on her phone.*

They all continue, RADHA, SIDDHARTHA *and* LILY, *the cricket game,* ISMET *and his Skype call. A gentle hubbub of life.*

Radha's landline rings. She looks to it.

A Sri Lankan woman, OLD NIHINSA, *enters, sweeping the stage.*

We are now in …

SCENE SIX

Colombo. The front porch of a grand old house on Milagiriya Avenue.

OLD NIHINSA *sweeps the porch.*

SUNIL *enters, moving down onto the front porch. He's on the phone. He carries a book. He drinks whiskey.*

SUNIL: So the Pandavas and the Kauravas—the two great families of the land—face each other, ready for battle. Arjuna is the Pandava's greatest warrior. Lord Krishna, his charioteer, readies his conch for the battle cry. And—just at this moment—Arjuna falters. He has gurus, friends, relations on the other side of the battle line. How can he kill his own teachers? His own flesh and blood? And *here* my Italian friend is where Krishna reveals himself in his cosmic manifestation. He shares his divine wisdoms with Arjuna. 'Do not yield to unmanliness, O, son of Pritha, it does not become you.' This is the famous Baghavad Gita. I have been re-reading it during the ceasefire. What else is there to do? [*He sits down.*] Krishna says a man's fate is determined by his talents. If one is gifted at a certain thing, that is one's path. That is how our fates are decided. [*Beat.*] We both know that this ceasefire is about to end. It is time to continue *our* fates. The Chinese will continue to give their satellite data to the government, the Ukranians will continue to give their tanks to both sides, the Americans will sell cluster bombs to fit in the Italian planes and then my friend, then my client will continue to buy from the Italians, and the Italians *must* continue to sell. That is *our* particular path. What will be the whole, manifold outcome? No-one can say. It is all *maya* anyway, my Italian friend. Illusion. A cosmic game. We each do our little bit. The rest is not up to us. [*Beat.*] Of course, a certain *price* is put on all this uncertainty. That price will cost my client and it will profit you and I. This is understood. [*Listening.*] Three percent. [*Listening.*] Yes. [*Listening.*] My client will agree to that. [*Listening.*] Yes.

> *He continues to listen as* THIRRU *enters.*

No no no, I may be a Tamil but remember my friend I am from India. *Not* Sri Lanka. I am separated from all that business my friend. Cleeeeeanly separated. At a certain point I will leave the discussion. My client has an agent who will take delivery.

THIRRU: That's not your chair.

> OLD NIHINSA *sees* THIRRU. *She walks towards him.*

SUNIL: [*phone*] My apologies— would you hold for a moment? Nihinsa? යන්න ... බලන්න ... අර හිඟන මිනිහා. (Go to that beggar, will you?)

OLD NIHINSA: Thirru?

> THIRRU *turns to* OLD NIHINSA *and nods.* OLD NIHINSA *faints.*

THIRRU: Nihinsa!

> *He goes to her. He speaks in Sinhala to* OLD NIHINSA—*the lines are not translated into English.*

> *Overlapping:*

Nihinsa …

OLD NIHINSA: / [*recovering, touching his face*] තිරූ ... ඇත්තටම ඔයා ද? (Thirru? Is that you?)

Left to right: Antonythasan Jesuthasan and Sukania Venugopal in the Belvoir/Co-Curious production. Photo: Brett Boardman.

SUNIL: / [*phone*] My deepest apologies my Italian friend but I must attend to a rather odd man on my porch.

THIRRU: / ඔව්. මම තමා. මොකද මේ? කෝ රාධා? (Yes. It's me. What's going on? Where is everyone?) Who is that man?

SUNIL: / [*phone*] Nothing to worry about, I'm sure. I will call again in half an hour.

> SUNIL *hangs up.*

මොනවද? මොනවද දෙන්නා කතා කරන්නෙ? (What are you two talking about?) Who do you think you are, මගේ ගේ ඇතුළට එන්ඩ? (barging into my house?)

> OLD NIHINSA *watches discreetly.*

THIRRU: [*turning to* SUNIL] What happened to my wife and son?

SUNIL: I don't bloody know. Who are you? You speak English?

THIRRU: I do. What happened to my wife and son?

SUNIL: You are wasting my time. Get out of here, you dog—

THIRRU: My name is Thirru. My wife is Radha. And this is our home.

SUNIL: [*pause*] *Thirru?* You're dead. Radha told me you were dead—

THIRRU: When did she tell you that?

> THIRRU *takes* SUNIL *by the shoulders.*

SUNIL: / Calm down.

THIRRU: / Where is my wife? Where is my son? What happened to my family?

SUNIL: / Calm down. Sssh. Listen … Listen. Listen.

> *Awkwardly,* SUNIL *releases himself.*

This *was* your home. It's mine now. [*Beat*] Radha sold this house to me. And then she left—

THIRRU: No—

SUNIL: As I said. She thought you were dead.

THIRRU: [*terrified at all the possible answers*] Where did she go?

SUNIL: Australia, I believe.

> *Pause.*

THIRRU: Radha would never leave / Sri Lanka—

SUNIL: / Thirru—

THIRRU: / She would have stayed—

SUNIL: Thirru. She left.

> HASANGA *rushes onto the porch.*

HASA: Thirru! Thank God!

SUNIL: For God's sake, not another one—

THIRRU: Hasa?

HASA: [*to* SUNIL] This man needs to go inside the house. Now. Get him away from the street, you idiot.

> HASA *begins to drag* THIRRU *into the house.*

SUNIL: What are you doing? Get out of my house!

HASA: I know who you are Sunil. I know what you do. Step back.

> SUNIL *steps back.*

Go back to the porch and keep reading your book. Whoever comes and whoever they are looking for tell them to get lost, you have no idea what they are talking about. Okay?

SUNIL: I think I might need more information than that—

HASA: Do you want this to become your problem?

SUNIL: Moorooha help us all! You have five minutes. That's it.

> HASA *takes* THIRRU *into the house.*

> SUNIL *sits on the porch and opens his book.*

Normal ඉන්න okay? (Behave normally. Okay?)

> OLD NIHINSA *does not move.*

Normal ඉන්න! (Behave normally!)

> OLD NIHINSA *sweeps the floor.*

HASA: I hoped that you would come here. I could not be there Thirru, at the jail. I could not be seen with you when you got out.

THIRRU: Hasa—

HASA: We thought you were dead. So many were dead. So many were missing.

THIRRU: Hasa—

HASA: And then with the ceasefire— I saw a list. I saw your name on an Amnesty list. I almost had a heart attack! I applied some political pressure and organised your passage from the camps to a jail in Colombo—

THIRRU: Hasanga!

> *Beat.*

> *You* freed me?

HASA: Yes.

THIRRU: Thank you.

HASA: You are free, Thirru.

THIRRU: Yes. Thank you.

HASA: Thirru, listen to me.

THIRRU: Thank you.

HASA: Listen to me carefully. [*Beat.*] Your father was killed in crossfire in the Elephant Pass battle in '96. Your mother was teaching at a school when it was hit by an aerial missile, three years ago. I'm sorry, Thirru.

> *Beat.*

THIRRU: Within weeks of imprisoning me, my jailor told me that he was willing to make contact with my parents. I gave him the details of my cousin, who could ask after them. They killed him and his family. My jailor relayed this news to me gleefully. [*He looks straight at Hasa.*] Tell me. Would you try and contact your family if you knew *that* could happen to them?

HASA: I would rather rot in jail than be the cause of my own parents' deaths.

THIRRU: Thank you. Thank you for saying that.

> *Pause.*

HASA: Thirru—Radha is in Australia. She is safe. She has a job. She has not, as far as I know, remarried. I believe she is now an Australian citizen. She lives in a small apartment in Pendle Hill—a suburb in Sydney. There are many other Sri Lankans there. I have her number. I have her email address. Her street address. Here.

> HASA *holds out a small piece of paper.* THIRRU *takes it, puts it in his shirt pocket.*

You have a son. One son. Siddhartha. He's twenty-one years old. He's studying journalism. No influence of mine, I swear. [*Beat.*] I haven't told her, Thirru. I haven't told Radha about you. I haven't told anyone. As I said, I didn't believe it was true until now. Listen,

Thirru. The first thing you have to do is call her. You have to call her.

THIRRU: Of course.

HASA: And you need to make a decision.

THIRRU: I have been thinking about this moment for many, many years Hasa.

HASA: And?

POLICEMAN: [*to* SUNIL] ඒයි! (Hey! You!)

> *A low level* POLICEMAN *appears at the front porch.* THIRRU *and* HASA *pause.* OLD NIHINSA *watches the action with* SUNIL:

SUNIL: Um—yes? Hello?

POLICEMAN: සිංහල බෑ? (You can't speak Sinhala?)

SUNIL: පොඩ්ඩක් තමයි. (Very little.) Can you speak Tamil?

POLICEMAN: No. [*Beat.*] Where are your guests?

SUNIL: Excuse me?

POLICEMAN: Where are your guests?

SUNIL: No guests. I am alone here.

POLICEMAN: You don't have guests? Any—visitors, I mean. Any visitors? No-one has turned up here?

> *He peers into the house.*

SUNIL: I haven't the faintest idea what you are talking about.

POLICEMAN: We are looking for a man. Thirru Sivakumar. You must call our number when you see him. [*He gives him a card.*] He will come. Here. Today.

SUNIL: Yes of course, of course I will. Thank you for warning me.

POLICEMAN: [*beat*] I will search the house now.

SUNIL: No.

POLICEMAN: Excuse me?

SUNIL: Not unless you have good reason to do so.

POLICEMAN: I have good reason to do so.

SUNIL: [*beat*] Here.

> SUNIL *offers him a bribe. The* POLICEMAN *takes it. Then:*

POLICEMAN: Nice watch, Sir.

> *He holds his hand out for more.*

> SUNIL *points to a house across the road.*

SUNIL: අර ගෙදර ... See that? Your commander's house. Commander, Indian ambassador, මම ... විස්කි ගැහුවා, last night, you know. (See that man's house? That is your commander's house. I drank whiskey with him and the Indian ambassador last night.)

POLICEMAN: Sir.

The POLICEMAN *goes.*

SUNIL *goes inside.*

SUNIL: You both need to leave this house as soon as possible.

HASA: This was his house.

SUNIL: [*pointing at Thirru*] That man is putting us all in danger. He needs to go.

HASA: We will leave when we are ready to leave.

SUNIL: Why are you helping him? You're Singhalese, he's Tamil.

HASA: We are Sri Lankan.

SUNIL: Leave. Now.

HASA: You have been selling arms to the government on one side and the Tigers on the other.

Beat.

SUNIL: Leave or I will call my associates.

HASA: My newspaper has been following you. We can publish the story on the front page of the *Leader* tomorrow morning. Which associates will you call?

SUNIL: [*realising*] You're that Hasa fellow. The editor of the *Leader*.

HASA: Yes. I am.

SUNIL: One day someone will kill you.

HASA: Someone will kill you tomorrow if I publish that story.

Beat.

SUNIL: There's nothing more dangerous than a ceasefire. [*Beat*] It's all *maya* anyway. One hour. That's all.

HASA: Come. [*He motions to* SUNIL] Bring the phone inside. [*To* THIRRU] Sunil is right. You are in danger. This is what they do— they accept bribes to release you and then come back to re-imprison you. I won't find you a second time, Thirru. I'm going to send you up North / until this all settles—

THIRRU: / Hasa—

HASA: Apah once took me to a place in the Vanni, deep in the jungles. There is a small / temple there where you can hide—

THIRRU: I must go, Hasa. I must go to my family.

HASA: There is a way to survive here Thirru. Not just survive. To *live*.

THIRRU: Even if I am hiding in the Northern-most tip of this island, I will not be safe.

HASA: I understand, but we—

THIRRU: Hasa— I must go to Australia—

HASA: You can't just go to Australia—

THIRRU: You said Radha is an Australian citizen—

HASA: This government will label you a terrorist. They're not going to give you a passport.

THIRRU: Hasa. I must see Radha. I must see Siddhartha.

Long pause.

HASA: There is another option. But it is risky.

THIRRU: Anything. Anything.

HASA: Flee.

THIRRU: I don't understand.

HASA: Claim what is known as your 'universal right against persecution'. Australia accepts people from countries all over the world who do this.

SUNIL: That is a very stupid idea.

THIRRU: Why?

HASA: There are risks. The journey can be slow. It's dangerous—

SUNIL: That is a severe understatement.

HASA: You probably won't make it to Australia.

THIRRU: But if I stay here they will kill me!

HASA: And even if you do make it there safely, there is a chance that they will just send you back to Sri Lanka.

THIRRU: But there is a chance that they would accept me?

HASA: Yes. As a refugee.

THIRRU: A *refugee*? Me?

Beat.

HASA: Yes.

Pause.

THIRRU: How do I do this?

Pause.

HASA: Thirru, I— If you go to the Australian High Commission they may tell the Sri Lankan Government … Leaving the island isn't easy. Look, I'm sorry, my connections aren't useful in this context. But this 'successful businessman'—

He looks pointedly at SUNIL.

THIRRU: Sunil. Could you organise something for me?

Pause.

What you said to the policeman, your connections …

SUNIL: Thirru—

THIRRU: Sunil. I lived here with Radha. This was her home. Her grandfather built it. He took me in. We were married here. I was supposed to raise my son here. Now everyone is gone except Nihinsa—and you. *You* have my house. I don't know what happened that day, but I know that Radha would never, *never* sell this house to a stranger.

Pause. THIRRU *takes the book from* SUNIL's *hand and holds it together with his own battered old book.*

'Charity given to a worthy person, simply because it is right, without consideration of anything in return, at the proper time and place, is considered the essence of goodness.' Baghavad Gita. Chapter seventeen, verse twenty.

Long pause.

SUNIL: I'll get you to India. Maybe Malaysia. Okay?

THIRRU: Thank you Sunil.

SUNIL: This is going to be very expensive. Do you own anything? Do you have access to any …

THIRRU *shakes his head.*

Beat.

SUNIL *exits.*

THIRRU: The jasmine plants, the temple trees—

HASA: They died in '83.

Pause.

Your arm …

THIRRU: I …

HASA: Okay. Not now.

> SUNIL *returns carrying several bundles of U.S. dollars.*

SUNIL: Take this.

HASA: [*sardonic*] My, what a profitable business you run, Sunil.

> THIRRU *accepts the gift.*

THIRRU: For Radha.

SUNIL: Precisely.

HASA: [*utterly serious*] You understand, you will probably die on the way?

THIRRU: I have been dead for twenty years.

> *Pause.*

I never thought that I would leave Sri Lanka.

HASA: I know.

THIRRU: I'm betraying my country, Hasa.

HASA: It's okay. [*He takes off the gold chain around his neck and gives it to* THIRRU.] Go, Thirru. Go.

> *All three men look at the phone that is sitting between them on the table.*

THIRRU: Hasa. Could you please start the call?

HASA: Of course.

THIRRU: Please, *machaan.* Call her for me. Tell her the news slowly. [*Beat.*] And then put me on the line.

> *The three men look at each other for a long moment. Then* HASA *reaches over to the phone and begins to dial.*

SCENE SEVEN

It is the same moment as at the end of Scene Five.

Radha's home phone is ringing. She answers.

RADHA: Hello?

HASA: Radha? Radha, it's Hasa here.

RADHA: Hasa? To what do I owe the honour of this call? Don't tell me you've finally found yourself a wife? She's probably much / younger than—

HASA: Radha.

Beat.

RADHA: What's wrong? Is it Nihinsa? Is she okay—

HASA: Radha … I found Thirru. I found him. He's here, Radha. Sitting next to me. He's alive.

Pause.

RADHA: Are you playing some stupid bloody trick on me?

HASA: I would never do something like that to you. I'm going to put him on, okay? Okay Radha?

HASA hands THIRRU the phone. He takes it.

THIRRU: Radha?

Pause.

Radha?

RADHA hangs up.

Pause.

THIRRU passes the phone back to HASA, who dials again.

RADHA listens to the phone ring.

She picks it up, but does not say anything.

HASA: Radha? Radha, don't hang up. It really is Thirru. He's been in prison. I found his name on a list. Radha, are you listening?

Pause.

TEENAGE RADHA and TEENAGE THIRRU run across the stage in bright white school clothes, chased by NIHINSA. Their clothes are a little soiled; twigs are in their hair. TEENAGE RADHA holds a handful of mangoes.

TEENAGE THIRRU: How many did you steal?!

NIHINSA: Thirru! Radha! Radha!

They exit.

APAH, old and grey, enters, using his walking stick for support.

RADHA *watches him.*

APAH: Why did you do it, darling? Why did you pick *him*?

> *Pause.*

HASA: Radha?
RADHA: Hasa?
HASA: Yes?
RADHA: Could you call back in thirty minutes?
HASA: … Radha. We might not be able to—
RADHA: *Hasa.*
HASA: … Okay. Okay, Radha. We'll do that.

> HASA *hangs up.*

> *Pause.* RADHA *holds onto the phone.*

END OF ACT ONE

ACT TWO

SCENE ONE

Milagiriya Avenue, Colombo. 1956.

The front porch of Apah's Colombo home. This is the same house we saw Thirru come home to in Act One. On the porch is the wooden armchair we last saw in Radha's Pendle Hill apartment.

It is early morning. The sound of crows and squirrels, the occasional bus or motorcycle horn. The gentle ocean underneath it all.

It is peaceful.

NIHINSA, *in her 30s, is sweeping the porch with a broom made of coconut fronds.*

APAH, *in his late 50s, sits with the* PRIEST. *They are wearing sarongs, bare-chested, eating stringhoppers, sothi and sambal.*

We watch them eat. Birds fly overhead. The men watch them pass.

APAH: ஞாயித்துக் கிழமை … ரோட்டில ஒரு சனம் இல்ல. கடல் அலை மட்டும் தான். (Sunday morning. No traffic. Just the ocean.)

> *They continue to eat.*
>
> APAH *suddenly stops eating and listens more intently.*

குழந்த ஒண்டிண்ட சத்தம் கேட்டது போல இருந்துது. (I thought I heard the baby.)

> DHAMAYANTHI *enters with baby* RADHA. AACHA *follows.*
>
> APAH *and the* PRIEST *rise to greet them.*

AACHA: Apah. No shouting. She's sleepy. [*To the* PRIEST] உப்புப் புளி எல்லாம் சரிதானே ஐயர்? (Not too much salt?)

PRIEST: பிரமாதம் … அருமையா இருக்கு! (It was perfect.)

> YOUNG DHAMAYANTHI *touches the* PRIEST*'s feet. He gives her his blessings.*

DHAMAYANTHI: Ayar. This is Radha.

PRIEST: Radha.

They gaze at baby RADHA.

PRIEST: Who does she take after?

DHAMAYANTHI: I think she looks just like her grandmother.

AACHA: And she has the temperament of her grandfather.

APAH: Chi. She is one day old!

They laugh.

APAH *begins to sing gently, an old Thevaram, Koothrayinavaaru. As he begins a second verse:*

AACHA: Apah. She's just fallen asleep. Dhamayanthi darling. Take Radha and yourself to the bedroom. Go and get some sleep. Go on, both of you.

DHAMAYANTHI *and baby* RADHA *exit.*

PRIEST: [*singing*] கொடுமைபல செய்தன நான்அறியேன். ('I must have done many misdeeds to feel so sick. I am ignorant, oh God.')

APAH: அறியாமை என்றது உங்களுக்குப் பொருந்தாது ஐயர். (You could hardly be called ignorant, Ayar.)

AACHA: தன்னை விட கூட தெரிஞ்ச ஆள் எண்டு, உங்கள மட்டுந்தான் என்ர புருஷன் சொல்லுவார். (You are the only person in this city that my husband will admit knows more than he does.)

PRIEST: *Chi chi chi.* If all the world's oceans were to hold all the knowledge there is, I would only know [*he holds up his water bowl*] but this much. Only the divine knows how it all fits together.

Offstage, the sound of a car horn.

சரி … நான் வெளிக்கிற்ற நேரமாச்சு. என்ர சகோதரம் என்ன சந்தைக்குக் கொண்டு போறன் எண்டு சொன்னவர். வேகமாகத்தான் வாகனத்தை ஓட்டுவார். (It's time. My brother is taking me to the market. He drives too fast.)

They all stand.

போயிட்டு வாறன். (See you soon.)

APAH: போயிட்டு வாங்கோ. (See you soon.)

The PRIEST *goes.*

AACHA: Nihinsa.

AACHA *and* NIHINSA *clean up.*

APAH *walks up and down the porch, looking out at the street.*

APAH: One equals zero point nine nine nine nine nine—

AACHA: Do not wake the baby.

APAH: Is the jasmine blooming early this year?

AACHA: Do you hear me?

APAH: I am not to wake the baby. [*Suddenly he yells out to the street.*] Bala!

BALA: [*offstage*] Apah!

AACHA: Shut up!

Overlapping:

APAH: [*yelling*] வா வா வா … எப்ப வந்தனீ கொழும்புக்கு. (Welcome back to Colombo! Come come come!)

BALA: [*offstage*] ஓம் அப்பா … இப்ப தான். (Thank you Apah, yes!)

AACHA: Nihinsa තේ වික්කරන්න. (Nihinsa, cups of tea.) Apah shut up.

NIHINSA *exits.*

APAH: Bala is back from Jaffna.

AACHA: I heard.

APAH: [*in a loud whisper*] You must buy all of his fruit. Pay him at *vellakaran* rates!

AACHA: Don't wake the baby!

She exits.

BALA *wheels in his fruit cart. He is a poor man in a sarong and simple shirt. His cart is laden with mangoes, papaya and bananas.*

APAH: பாலா … ஆச்சரியமா இருக்கு! (Bala! What a lovely surprise!)

BALA: வணக்கம் அப்பா … எப்பிடி சுகம்? (Good morning Apah! How are you?)

APAH: எனக்கென்னடா குறை. நான் இப்ப பேரன் ஆயீட்டன். Bloody marvellous. (I am a grandfather.)

BALA: ஆ … பிள்ள பிறந்திட்டுதா? (Very good, the baby has arrived?)

APAH: நேற்றுத்தான் பிறந்தவள்! (She was born yesterday! Utterly splendid.)

BALA: பெடியனோ, பெட்டையோ? (Boy or girl?)

APAH: பெடுச்சி. (Girl.)

BALA: பேர் வைச்சிட்டீனமே? (What is her name?)

APAH: ராதா. (Radha.)

BALA: ராதா ... நல்ல பெயர். (Radha. Beautiful.)

APAH: ஆள் நித்திரை ... வா ... இப்படி ஆச்சாவின்ர கதிரையில இரு. ... சொல்லு, இப்ப கொழும்பில என்ன செய்யிறாய்? (But she is asleep. [*He gestures, disappointed*] Come. Sit sit sit. Tell me. What are you doing in Colombo?)

BALA: நேற்றிரவு யாழ்ப்பணத்தில பஸ் ஏறின்னான். (I came on the overnight bus from Jaffna.)

APAH: Yes yes. You have come for business? [*Calls out*] Nihinsa! කෝප් ලෑස්කිද! (Nihinsa! Cups of tea!)

BALA: [*he smiles*] நாலிடத்தில சாமான் வாங்கிறம். வவுனியாவில இரண்டிடத்தில, நீர்கொழும்பில ஒருவனிட்ட, நான் இங்கால வர, கொழும்பில வாங்கிற ஆள் யாழ்ப்பாணம் போட்டுது. (I have four contractors now. Two in Vavuniya, one in Negombo, but my seller in Colombo has gone back North to Jaffna so I have the cart until my cousin finishes school.) I am business man now. Thank you Apah, thank you. [*He holds out an envelope to* APAH] Please. My first repayment on the loan.

APAH: சீ ... அடுத்த மாசமெல்லோ? (Chi. It's due next month.)

BALA: இல்ல ஐயா.. என்னட்ட கொஞ்சம் வந்திருக்குது. இப்பவே தரலாம். (Please. I'm happy to pay today.)

APAH: உனக்கு விருப்பமெண்டா தா ... ஆனா உன்னால ஏலுமெண்டால் மட்டும் தான். (If you're happy, fine, but do not give your money away to me until you are ready.)

BALA: ஏலும் ஐயா ... எல்லாம் உங்கண்ட உதவியால தான் நடக்குது. (Sir, I am ready. You made all this possible. Thank you.)

APAH *takes the envelope.*

அடுத்த வருஷம் நானே ஒரு கட தொடங்கப் போறன். (Maybe next year I will open a shop.)

NIHINSA *enters with tea.*

BALA: Hello, Nihinsa. How are your children?

NIHINSA: Good morning, Bala. හොඳින් ඉන්නවා කියලා තමයි අපේ අම්මලා කියන්නේ. ඒත සතියේ දිහාවට යන්න ඉන්නේ

ගමට, උන්ව බලලා එන්න. (Their grandparents say they are okay. Hopefully I'll be able to go down South next week to my village, to see my babies.)

APAH: ආච්චාට කියන්න නිහින්සට මේ සතිඅන්තේ ඇල්පිටියෙ යන්න දෙන්න කියලා! (Tell Aacha to let you go to Elpitiya this weekend!) [To BALA] தன்ர பிள்ளைகள் நல்லா இருக்கீணமாம். தேத்தண்ணி குடிப்பியே? (She says her children are okay. Tea?)

BALA: ஓம் ஜயா. (Thank you.)

NIHINSA: වැඩ එහෙම? හොඳයි? (How is your work going?)

APAH: She asks how is your business. [To NIHINSA] එයාට කොන්ත්‍රාත්කාරයෝ හතර දෙනෙක් ඉන්නවා ... දෙන්නෙක් උතුරේ— වවුනියාවේ, අනික් දෙන්නා මීගමුවෙයි කොළඹයි. (He has four contractors, two up North in Vavuniya, and two in Negombo and Colombo.)

BALA: அடுத்த வருஷம் நானே ஒரு கட தொடங்கப் போறன். (Maybe next year I will open a shop.)

APAH: සමහරවිට ලබන අවුරුද්දෙ කඩයක් අරියි. (And maybe next year he will open a shop.)

   AACHA *enters. Overlapping:*

AACHA: பாலா ... எப்ப வந்தனீ? சின்னவன் நல்லா இருக்கிறானே? (Bala! How's the little fellow?)

BALA: நல்ல சுகமா இருக்கிறான். ஆனா, கன கதை இல்லை. (He's healthy. Very quiet.)

AACHA: பிறகென்ன வேணும் உனக்கு ... கடவுளுக்கு நன்றி சொல்லு! (What more could you want? Thank the gods.)

BALA: ஓம் ஆச்சா. ஒவ்வொரு நாளும் நான் கும்புடுறனான். அது சரி, நீங்கள் பாட்டியாகீற்றீங்கள் எண்டு அப்பா சொன்னார். (I do, Aacha. Everyday. Apah tells me you have just become a grandmother?)

AACHA: ஓம் ஓம் ... வலு சந்தோஷம். அப்பா பெருசா ஏதோவெல்லாம் யோசிச்சு வைச்சிருக்கிறார். (Yes! We are very very proud. Apah has big plans.)

APAH: அவள் நல்ல கெட்டிக்காரி (She is extremely clever!)

AACHA: அவளுக்கு இன்னும் ஒரு நாள் முடியேல்ல ... என்ன வைச்சிருக்கிறாய் இண்டைக்கு? (She is one day old. What do you have today?)

BALA: சோக்கான பப்பாளிப்பழம் ... நம்ப மாட்டியள், நல்ல

இனிப்பு (Excellent papaya Aacha. Very sweet. You won't believe it.)

She examines the fruit.

APHA: இப்ப நாலு பேரோட வியாபாரம் ... அடுத்த வருஷம் அவருக்கெண்டு தனிக் கடை ... (He has four contractors now. Next year maybe a shop.)

BALA: நன்றி அப்பா. (Thank you to Apah.)

AACHA: பார்லிமண்டில இவற்ற சேட்டைகள் என்னென்ணடு எனக்குத் தெரியாது ... ஆனா உனக்கு ... அது சரி, அம்மா எப்பிடி இருக்கிறா? (I don't see the need for half the mischief he gets up to in Parliament but for you, okay. How is your mother?)

AACHA *cuts open a papaya.*

BALA: எவ்வளவோ பரவாயில்ல ஆச்சா ... கால் வீக்கம் நல்லா வத்தீட்டுது. டொக்டர் பாலேந்திரா நல்ல கெட்டிக்காரன். அவர் சொல்லச் சொன்னவர் அப்பா, உரும்பிராயில இருக்கிற கோப்பாய் பள்ளிக்கூடம் முழுசா எரிஞ்சுபோச்சு. (Much better, Aacha, thank you. Her feet aren't swollen anymore. Dr Balendra is a very clever man. He told me to tell you, Apah, the Kopay schoolhouse in Urumpirai burnt down.)

APAH: சத்தியமா எண்டு? (No!)

AACHA: Oh God.

BALA: They will make it an 'electronics' store—

APAH: / என்ன கொடூரமான செய்தி! (Terrible news!)

AACHA: பள்ளிக்கூடத்தைப் பற்றிச் சொல்லி அவரைக்கிளப்பிவிட வேண்டாம். (Don't get him started on that schoolhouse.)

APAH *stands and closes his eyes and recites with great formality:*

APAH: 'When two numbers are so combined, as that the one has always a unit answering to every unit of the other, we pronounce them *equal*.'

AACHA: There we go. [*Ignoring* APAH, *investigating the papaya*] Sweet. Very nice. Nihinsa, try.

APAH: Before the schoolhouse I had no mathematics.

AACHA: [*to* NIHINSA] පොල් හොද්ද බලන්න. හොදට හොලවලා බලන්න ... (Check the coconuts. Shake them, listen for water.)

APAH: Before mathematics I had no trousers. ஐயாவோடயும் அம்மாவோடயும் நெல்லு விதைச்சன் ... கிணத்தில இருந்து தண்ணி இறைச்சன் ... மாட்டுக்குச் சாப்பாடு போட்டன் ... சந்தோஷமா இருந்தன். சில நேரம் பயிரெல்லாம் பாழாப் போகும் ... மழை தேவைக்கு அதிகமாப் பெய்யும் ... சில நேரம் மழையே இல்லாமப் போகும். (Like my amma's amma's ammamma I sowed the paddy, trod the wellspring, fed the bullock. I was content. But then there was a bad crop. Too much rain, too little rain.)

BALA: அரிசி இல்லை— (No rice—)

APAH: கத்திரிக்காய் இல்லை— (No eggplant—)

BALA: மாம்பழம் இல்லை— (No mangoes—)

APAH: பிறகு பசியோட படுப்பம். சந்தோஷம் இல்லாமப் போகும். என்ன சொல்றாய் பாலா ... விவசாயிகளிண்ட வாழ்க்கை நல்ல வாழ்க்கை எண்டு நினைக்கிறியா? (And we go hungry. Then I am not content. Is the life of a farmer a good life, Bala?)

BALA: ஓமெண்டும் சொல்லலாம் ... இல்லை எண்டும் சொல்லலாம். (Yes, Apah. And no.)

APAH: ஓமெண்டும் சொல்லலாம் ... இல்லை எண்டும் சொல்லலாம் ... அதெண்டா சரி தான். அப்பிடித் தான் இருந்தது. ஒரு நாள் என்ர அம்மாவுக்கு ஒரு யோசனை வந்தது. பின்ன, ஒவ்வொரு நாளும் வயல் வேலையை முடிச்சுக் கொண்டு, மாட்டுக்குச் சாப்பாட்டை வைச்சிட்டு பள்ளிக்கூடத்துக்கு ஓடிப் போவன். (Yes and no. For a farmer, what is good is bad. How can this be so? But so it was, until one day my mother came across a new idea: school. The gossip was that 'school would get you trousered employment in the city'. So every morning, after the paddy and the wellspring and the bullock, I ran to the kopay—)

AACHA: ஏனப்பா புளுகுறீங்கள்? ஒவ்வொரு நாளும் பள்ளிக்கூடத்துக்கு ஓடியா போனனீங்கள்? (Please! You did not run to school every day.)

APAH: உண்மையில நான் வேகமா ஓடயில்ல எண்டு தான் சொல்ல வேணும். நான் வாங்கியிருக்கிற பிரம்படி தளும்புகளைப் பாத்திருக்கிறீர் தானே. (On the contrary! I didn't run fast enough! [*He points to his bottom*] You have seen my cane marks, no?)

AACHA: முருகா ... கணேஷா.. சிவ சிவா (Moorooha, Ganesha, /

Shiva …)

During the following VINSANDA, *in his 40s and dressed in a suit, enters unnoticed. He stays off the porch and listens.*

APAH: I ran from my village Urumpirai to the schoolhouse in Kopay, from the paddy field to the algebraic equation. 'If one always has a unit answering to every unit of the other, we pronounce them equal.' Bala, the algebraic equation changed my life. Before the algebraic equation, what was good was bad. Yes and no. But algebra is not like that. In algebra, one is always one. Two minus one is / always one.

AACHA: Shut up and eat, Apah.

APAH: The square root of four, times the square root of four, divided by four, is always one. The principle of equality means that whatever is given to one side is also given to the other. One unit here is equal to one unit there. Any number of units here is equal to any number of units there. One side can change in endless motion but the requirement is always equality. My amma saw this, Bala. She saw my excitement and she let me go. A poor Tamil boy from the North, she let me go to the schoolhouse in Kopay, to a boarding school in Colombo, to Trinity College Cambridge, to the Parliament of Ceylon. Is this not my life? And is this not our country, Bala? Is this not Ceylon? Nihinsa, what is the Sinhala word for equal?

NIHINSA: සමානයි. (Equal.)

APAH: And Bala, what is the Tamil word for equal?

BALA: சமன். (Equal.)

APAH: සමානයි and சமன். [*English*] You see? It is a universal value.

VINSANDA: If he's not eating he's talking, if he's not talking he's eating.

Overlapping:

APAH: Vinsanda! Come come come. Join us for breakfast!

AACHA: Morning Vinsanda.

VINSANDA: Morning.

APAH: I am a grandfather!

AACHA: Stop shouting!

VINSANDA: I know, you telephoned me yesterday. Congratulations. I'm thrilled for you.

AACHA: Just one month younger than your Hasa. Maybe when they are older we can get them together, hey?

APAH: She is one day old.

AACHA: Perfect time! We must speak to the astrologer. When exactly was Hasa born? I will find out his / *nakshatra*—

APAH: Aacha! [*To* VINSANDA] Stop standing over there, come and eat.

VINSANDA: Thank you for the invitation, but on this particular day I should probably stay over here.

APAH: Ah. You visit as a colleague, not as a friend.

VINSANDA: I do.

APAH: I see.

AACHA: *Chi.* Who left a stringhopper on the ground?

VINSANDA: Bandaranaike began his election campaign yesterday. He spoke at a rally in Elpitiya—

APAH: That is Nihinsa's village. [*To* NIHINSA] ආරංචිද? බණ්ඩාරීගේ ඇල්පිටියෙ කතාවක් කරලා. (Do you know this? Banda spoke in Elpitiya yesterday.)

NIHINSA: ඔව් ලොකු මහත්තය. අපේ එක්කෙනා ගිහින් තිබ්බා. (Sir. Yes. My husband was there.)

VINSANDA: එයා කිව්වද උඹට බණ්ඩා මොනවද කිව්වේ කියලා? (Did he tell you what Banda said?)

APAH: කවදා ඉදන්ද උඹේ මිනිහ බණ්ඩගේ රැලි වලට යන්න ගත්තේ? (When did your husband start going to Banda's rallies?)

BALA: அப்பா.. இதென்ன … பண்டாவின்ர புது கொள்கையை பற்றியா? (Please, Apah. Is this about Banda's new policy?)

AACHA: Where are my glasses?

NIHINSA: / ලොකු මහත්තය, බණ්ඩාරනායක මහත්තය, භාෂාව වෙනස් කරන්න හදනවලු. (Banda, Sir, wants to change the language.)

APAH: [*to* BALA] தெரியேல்ல. (I don't know.) [*To* NIHINSA] මොකද්ද උඹ කිව්වේ? (What did you say?)

Simultaneously:

NIHINSA: / බණ්ඩාරනායක මහත්තයට ඕනෙ රාජ්‍ය භාෂාව වෙනස් කරන්නලු. (Banda Sir wants to change the official language to Sinhala.)

BALA: பண்டா அரச கரும மொழிய சிங்களமா மாத்தப் போறார் (Bandaranaike wants to change the official language to Sinhala.)

VINSANDA: What did he say?

APAH: The same as she said.

AACHA: No politics in my house!

Beat.

APAH: Does Banda really want to change the official language to Sinhala?

VINSANDA: He's making his move against us.

AACHA: What did I just say?

VINSANDA: My apologies, Aacha, for disturbing you. But I must speak with your husband.

Beat.

AACHA: You can talk on the porch. If you are quiet. Radha is asleep. And don't be long. [*To* APAH] Behave yourself.

AACHA *whispers in* NIHINSA*'s ear.* NIHINSA *exits.*

AACHA *takes the tea and exits.*

The following is in English unless otherwise indicated.

APAH: Banda is the opposition leader now, of course he's making his move against us. But how can he change the language? It is what it is. Bala speaks Tamil. Nihinsa speaks Sinhala. And the official language is English.

VINSANDA: Banda calls it the Sinhala Only Policy.

APAH: A policy is just a policy! Come up on the porch, don't stand over there.

VINSANDA: He will change the official language from English to Sinhala. Sinhala *only*.

APAH: அவர் நாட்ட மாத்தாம, மொழிய மாத்த ஏலாது. (He cannot change the language without changing Sri Lanka.)

VINSANDA: You know I cannot argue with you in Tamil.

APAH: உமக்குக் குடுத்து வைச்சது அவ்வளவு தான். பாலா? (Bad luck for you. Bala?)

BALA: [*to* VINSANDA] He says bad luck you.

NIHINSA *enters with a collared shirt, which* APAH *puts on.*

VINSANDA: Bad luck our party. Have you seen Banda's rallies? The crowds are massive.

APAH: His crowds are substantial but Banda still has to win the election.

Until then, we are the government, English is the official language and all Sri Lankans will speak their own language.

VINSANDA: I don't think you are taking this seriously.

APAH: It is ridiculous, I cannot take it seriously.

VINSANDA: It is clever politics.

APAH: What do you think Bala?

Beat.

BALA: [*English*] Mister Vinsanda.

VINSANDA: Yes?

APAH *simultaneously translates for* BALA.

BALA: இலங்கைக்கு இரண்டு மொழிகள் இருக்குது, அதோட, ஆங்கிலமும் இருக்குது. ஒருத்தர் தன்ர சொந்த மொழியை மட்டும் படிக்கப் போறாரா இல்ல மூண்டு மொழிகளையும் படிக்கப் போறாரா எண்டது அவரவற்ற விருப்பம். ஆனா எல்லாரும் இலங்கையர்கள் தான். என்ர மகன் ஆங்கிலப் பள்ளிக்கூடத்தில படிச்சு, நிஹின்ஸாவின்ர மகனும் ஆங்கிலப் பள்ளிக்கூடத்துக்குப் போனால், இரண்டு பேரும் ஒரு நல்ல கவர்மேந்து வேலையில சேரலாம். ஒருவன் தமிழ், ஒருவன் சிங்களம் ஆனா இரண்டு பேரும் இலங்கையர் தான். அது தான் இலங்கை. (Sri Lanka has two mother tongues, and English. Whether one stays with their own language or learns all three, they are still Sri Lankan. If my son, God willing, can go to school in English or Nihinsa's son chooses to go to school in English, both can find a very good job, both can become a public servant. One is Tamil, one is Sinhala, but both Sri Lankan. That is Sri Lanka.)

APAH: You see. Two languages equals one country.

VINSANDA: Fine words won't win the election.

APAH: The louder the radical voices of the opposition, the louder we must proclaim our place in the centre. We are the United National Party.

VINSANDA: The problem is not that the opposition are loud. The problem is that they are popular. Bandaranaike is building a nationalistic fervour—

APAH: A radical fervour.

VINSANDA: A popular, nationalistic fervour. නිහින්සා මොකද හිතන්නේ බණ්ඩාරනායක ගැන? ලබන පාර ෂන්දෙ දාන්නේ

එයාටද? අපිටද? (Nihinsa. What do you think of Bandaranaike? Will you vote for him in the upcoming elections? Or will you vote for us?)

NIHINSA *hesitates.*

APAH: ඇත්ත කියපන්. (Speak honestly.)

NIHINSA: ලොකු මහත්තයා, මං ... මං කැමතියි බණ්ඩාරනායක මහත්තයට. (I ... I like Bandaranaike, Sir.)

APAH: ඒ කියන්නෙ අපිට නිහින්සගේ ඡන්දෙ නැතිවුනා? (So we have lost your vote?)

NIHINSA: ඔව්. මම ඡන්දෙ දෙන්නේ බන්ඩාරනායක මහත්තයට. (Yes. I will vote for Bandaranaike, Sir.)

APAH: ඇයි? (Why?)

NIHINSA: අපේ පවුලේ හුඟක් අයට රස්සාවක් හොයාගන්න බෑ ... ඉංග්‍රීසි දන්නෙ නැත්තං ගොඩක් අමාරුයි රස්සා හොයාගන්න. අපි සුද්දෝ එළවගත්තට පස්සේ අපිට පොරොන්දු වුණේ රට හොඳ අතට හැරේවි කියලනේ ... මොකුත් වෙනස් වෙලා නෑ ලොකු මහත්තයා අපිට නං. බණ්ඩාරනායක මහත්තය පොරොන්දු වෙනවා සිංහල රස්සා දෙන්න. මහත්තය අපේ ගමට ආවා. අපේ පුංචි ගමට. කවුරුන් මීට කලින් එහෙම ඇවිත් නෑ. ඇවිත් සිංහලෙන් කතාකරා. අපේ භාෂාවෙන්. බහුතර භාෂාවෙන්. කවුරුවත් මීට කලින් එහෙම කරලා නෑ. බණ්ඩාරනායක මහත්තයා ආවොත් දැන්වත් මේක ... අපේ ආණ්ඩුවක් වෙයි. (Many in my family cannot find work, it is very hard if you do not know English. After we got rid of the British we were promised the country would finally change. Nothing has changed, Sir. Not for us. Bandranaike Sir promises Sinhala jobs. Bandaranaike Sir visited our village. Our little village. No-one has ever done that before. He spoke in Sinhala. Our language. The majority language. No-one has ever done that before. Finally with Bandaranaike this is … this is our government.)

VINSANDA: You see? Banda is on the march.

APAH: We have failed the poor Vinsanda, Sinhala *and* Tamil. *That* will be our new policy—to lift up *all* the poor. We must pronounce both sides equal—

VINSANDA: Apah. Listen to me. The Cabinet has met.

APAH: No it has not. I am the Trade Minister. I didn't meet.

VINSANDA: You were meeting your granddaughter—

APAH: Who is not in the Cabinet. The Cabinet did not meet.

VINSANDA: Apah. Listen. [*Beat.*] The United National Party has decided to adopt the key positions of the Sinhala Only Policy.

APAH: What kind of a United National Party is Sinhala only? I am Tamil.

VINSANDA: Yes. The *only* Tamil in Cabinet. And you must vote with Cabinet to adopt the key positions—

APAH: I will never do that.

VINSANDA: I know, I told this to the Cabinet.

APAH: The Prime Minister / will support me—

VINSANDA: I told this to the Prime Minister.

> *Beat.*

APAH: The stupid man wants me to resign from Cabinet?

> *Pause.* VINSANDA *looks at* APAH.

From the *party*?

VINSANDA: The Prime Minister will welcome you back to the party and the Cabinet after the election.

> *Pause.*

APAH: Do you agree with him?

VINSANDA: We must win the election.

APAH: Two languages, one country. One language, two countries.

VINSANDA: This is politics, not mathematics.

APAH: I will not leave Parliament.

VINSANDA: Then you be a party of one.

APAH: If I leave the United National Party I will have no choice but to attack the United National Party.

VINSANDA: Then we will attack you.

APAH: You will not find your way back to the centre.

VINSANDA: The Cabinet has decided.

APAH: This is stupidity! We must pronounce both sides / equal—

VINSANDA: Enough Apah! You don't listen. We cannot lose this election!

APAH: [*shouting*] We cannot lose our minds to win it either!

Offstage, a baby starts crying.

Bugger it to bloody hell.

AACHA: [*offstage, a scream*] Apah!

Beat.

APAH: [*to* BALA] அரசாங்கம் உன்ர மகனுக்கு ஆங்கிலத்தில படிப்பிக்காது எண்டால், நான் அதைச் செய்யிறன். (If the government won't give your son an education in English, I will.)

BALA: அப்பா (Apah?)

APAH: [*to* NIHINSA] නිහින්සා මේක බාලාට දෙන්න. (Nihinsa, please give this to Bala.) [*To* BALA] இந்தா அதுக்கான முதல்பணம். நான் மனச மாத்திறதா இல்ல. (Consider this a downpayment. Take it, I will not change my mind.)

NIHINSA *hands the envelope of cash to Bala.*

BALA: நன்றி அப்பா. (Thank you Apah.)

VINSANDA: What are you two talking about?

APAH: None of your business.

AACHA *enters with* DHAMAYANTHI *and baby* RADHA.

At the same time, RADHA *enters and sits in Aacha's chair.*

AACHA *slaps* APAH *on the head.*

Overlapping:

AACHA: Honestly.

VINSANDA: Dhamayanthi! Congratulations!

DHAMAYANTHI: Hello Vinsanda Mama.

VINSANDA: Hello little one!

DHAMAYANTHI: This is Radha.

VINSANDA: / Aren't you gorgeous?

AACHA: / [*handing money to* BALA] பப்பாப் பழத்துக்கும் தேங்காய்க்கும். (For the papaya and coconuts.)

VINSANDA: / Welcome to Sri Lanka!

BALA: ஆச்சா … தேவைக்கு அதிகமா தாறீங்கள். (Aacha, that is too much!)

AACHA: விசர்க் கதை … சந்தையில இந்த விலைக்குத்தான் விக்கிறாங்கள். (Nonsense. It is the market rate.) Vinsanda are you going to your silly bloody cricket game today?

VINSANDA: If you mean Sri Lanka's first ever test match against India, yes of course.

AACHA: What time does it bloody start?

VINSANDA: [*laughs, taking the hint*] Very bloody soon. I must go. [*Handing* DHAMAYANTHI *a small gift*] My wife prepared some *kithul* for you. Hide it from Apah.

DHAMAYANTHI: Thank you Vinsanda.

AACHA: Next time bring your Hasa to meet Radha.

VINSANDA: Absolutely. [*To* APAH] See you at the cricket, Apah.

Beat.

APAH: See you at the cricket.

VINSANDA *wobbles his head goodbye and exits.*

AACHA: [*to* DHAMAYANTHI] Go eat, child. Nihinsa, please.

NIHINSA *and* DHAMAYANTHI *exit.*

Vinsanda is right. You don't listen.

APAH: Did you know about Banda's speech?

AACHA: All you had to do was not wake the baby. Instead you have launched a political war against your own party at the beginning of an election campaign. [*Beat.*] Yes of course I knew. Stop sulking and come and eat.

APAH: In a moment.

She exits.

APAH *and* BALA *are alone. They speak in Tamil.*

உன்ர மகன நல்லதொரு பள்ளிக்கூடத்துக்கு நான் அனுப்புறன். அந்தப் பள்ளிக் கூடத்தை நான் தான் கட்ட வேணுமெண்டால், அதையும் நான் செய்வன். (I will send your son to a schoolhouse, even if I have to build it myself.)

BALA: ஓம் அப்பா. (Yes, Apah.)

APAH: ஒரு பக்கம் எப்பயும் இன்னொரு பக்கத்துக்குச் சமன். (One side is always equal to the other.)

BALA: ஓம் அப்பா. (Yes, Apah.)

APAH: மனனின்ர பேரென்ன? (What is your son's name?)

BALA: திரு. (Thirru.)

THIRRU *enters.*

APAH: திரு ... நல்லது. (Thirru. Very good.)

SCENE TWO

Sydney, 2004. The same as the end of Act One:
RADHA *by the phone in her Pendle Hill apartment.*
THIRRU, HASA *and* SUNIL *by the phone in Colombo.* NIHINSA *sweeping.*
SIDDHARTHA *rushes into Radha's house.*

SIDDHARTHA: Amma?
RADHA: Siddhartha. Sit down.
SIDDHARTHA: Amma, what's wrong?

> *Pause.*

RADHA: Siddhartha. Your father is alive.

> *Pause.*

He called earlier tonight, from Sri Lanka.

> *Pause.*

I asked him to call again. When you were here.

> *Pause.*

SIDDHARTHA: What?
RADHA: I'm not talking to him.

> *Long pause.*

The last time I spoke to your father ... he died.
SIDDHARTHA: Amma ...

> *Beat.*

RADHA: We must wait for his call.

> *They wait.*
>
> HASA *dials a long number on the phone.*
>
> *Radha's phone rings. She doesn't move.*
>
> SIDDHARTHA *answers, putting it on speakerphone.*

Beat.

HASA: Radha?

SIDDHARTHA: A … Ap …

HASA: Siddhartha? This is Hasa. I'm a friend of your mother's. We talked once when you were about … eleven years old.

SIDDHARTHA: Um—

HASA: I'm putting your father on. Hold on. [*To* THIRRU] It is Siddhartha on the phone.

HASA *hands* THIRRU *the phone.*

SIDDHARTHA: Ah …

THIRRU: சித்தார்த்தா … சித்தார்த்தாவா கதைக்கிறது? (Siddhartha? Is that you?)

SIDDHARTHA: Sorry, I— I can't speak Tamil.

THIRRU: Oh. Well, I can speak English.

SIDDHARTHA: Um. Amma just told me. A minute ago.

THIRRU: Right.

Beat.

SIDDHARTHA: Amma's not talking to you.

Beat.

THIRRU: I see.

They wait.

SIDDHARTHA: Thirru?

THIRRU: Yes, Siddhartha?

SIDDHARTHA: Can I be honest with you?

THIRRU: I suppose so.

SIDDHARTHA: As far as I'm concerned … you don't exist.

THIRRU: Yes. [*Beat.*] Can I be honest with you then, Siddhartha?

SIDDHARTHA: Go on.

THIRRU: I feel much the same way about you.

SUNIL: For God's sake, hurry up Thirru!

THIRRU: Son. I need to ask you something. Would that be okay?

SIDDHARTHA: Yes?

THIRRU: I would like to come to Australia. [*Beat.*] I don't know how yet, but—

SIDDHARTHA: What do you mean?

THIRRU: The government can't know that I'm leaving—
SIDDHARTHA: I don't understand—
THIRRU: And there isn't much time. I'm in danger, you see—
SIDDHARTHA: Right—
THIRRU: There's a man here, he's going to help me, his name is Sunil.

RADHA *suddenly stands and walks to the far side of the room.*

Overlapping:

SIDDHARTHA: [*looking at* RADHA] Who is Sunil—
THIRRU: Probably I will go to India first—
SIDDHARTHA: [*to* RADHA] Amma? Who is Sunil?
THIRRU: There are camps there—
SIDDHARTHA: [*to* THIRRU] Sorry, where? Fuck. Sorry—
THIRRU: In India.
SIDDHARTHA: What?
THIRRU: In India.
SIDDHARTHA: Right. Sorry. What camps?
THIRRU: Refugee camps.
SIDDHARTHA: Oh. [*Beat*] Okay. Then?
THIRRU: We haven't figured that out yet.
SIDDHARTHA: Right. So you'll call us? From India?
THIRRU: Yes, I—
SIDDHARTHA: What's your mobile number?
THIRRU: [*looking to* HASA] Mobile?
HASA: Tell him you'll use a calling card.
THIRRU: I'll call you using a— a calling card once we've decided our
    plan. I'll try and call in the evenings, Australian time. When you'll
    be at home, after work. Okay?
SIDDHARTHA: Ah. I don't ... I don't live at home.
THIRRU: You don't live at home?! Why?

Beat.

Is Radha *alone* there?

Beat.

Sorry, it's none of my business.

Pause.

Is there another number I should ring?

    Beat. SIDDHARTHA *looks at* RADHA. *She refuses to look at him.*

SIDDHARTHA: No. You should call here. I can be here.

THIRRU: You can?

SIDDHARTHA: I'll be here. I'll try to be here most nights.

THIRRU: Okay. Thank you.

SUNIL: For God's sake, finish the call!

THIRRU: [*to* SIDDHARTHA] Siddhartha. I have to go. Look. I'm going to leave Sri Lanka. Your mother … She didn't say *not* to come. I would listen to her advice, Siddhartha.

    SIDDHARTHA *looks at* RADHA. *She refuses to look at him.*

SIDDHARTHA: Okay.

THIRRU: Siddhartha?

SIDDHARTHA: Yes.

THIRRU: You can also tell me not to come.

    Pause.

Okay then.

    THIRRU *hands the phone to* HASA *who hangs it up.*

SUNIL: Let's go. Now. Now!

    SUNIL *quickly ushers them out.*

    SIDDHARTHA *hangs up.*

SIDDHARTHA: Then: nothing. A week. No calls. Nothing. Amma too. Not a word. Every night at six o'clock I catch a bus to Bondi Junction then a train to Pendle Hill and I let myself in. The room smells like mustard seeds and curry leaves. We put the TV on and wait for the phone to ring. Amma cooks but she doesn't speak. At midnight I catch the last train back to Bondi. I sit on the beach and watch the waves crash. Two weeks. I scour Google Maps for refugee camps. Menik Farm, Kalimoddai, Vembakottai. I show news articles to Amma. Is that him? The man who says he is my father? She shakes her head. She doesn't speak. I start running. Laps up and down the hills at Clovelly. Lily calls. We spend too much at Icebergs. We kiss on the beach. Rajapalayam, Mannar, Pulal. Four weeks. Nothing. Six o'clock. Pendle Hill station. Mutton curry with eggplant. *Australian Idol.* Manufacturing celebrities. The phone rings. It's telemarketers. Not the man who says he is my father. Midnight. Home. Lily can't stand the cold in Sydney, she curls up on my chest. At four a.m. I fall asleep. Five weeks. Every day I run. Casey Donovan wins the final with 'Come Fly With Me' and Amma cries. I take her hand, she gets up to wash the dishes. Not a word. Lily talks on the phone to her mum back home for hours in a language I don't understand. I run till it hurts. The phone rings. More telemarketers. Professional simulations. I scream at them. When I leave at night I see Amma through the window. She sits in Ammamma's chair. Silent. The lights are always on. My ears burn in the cold. Six weeks.

Cheddikulam, Nellikulam, Madurai Uchipatti. Amma sits in Ammamma's chair. Seven weeks. Eight weeks.

There are one hundred and thirty-two refugee camps just in India. What is this world? Are we animals or are we citizens? We are parents and children who have never met. *Simulacrums.* Water and water. Running water …

> *The sound of baila music.* AACHA *and two* YOUNG WOMEN *in sarees dance onto the stage.*
>
> SIDDHARTHA *runs and runs.*
>
> *The stage fills with people dancing.*
>
> RADHA *remains in Aacha's chair, still and silent.*
>
> SIDDHARTHA *runs through the audience and leaves.*
>
> *The music and dance becomes a great hubbub of Sri Lankan life—*

SCENE THREE

Milagiriya Avenue, Colombo, 1977.

Apah and Aacha's house. A wedding.

NIHINSA *and a* MALE SERVANT *walk through the audience, serving food.*

We are on the porch: a thoroughfare between wedding preparations inside the home and the wedding in the front yard. People cross through the space throughout the scene.

At the centre of it all, for the entire scene, RADHA *remains in Aacha's chair.*

A HOPPER MAN (*Sri Lankan crepes man*) *wheels his cart on.*

AACHA: எங்க போறாய்? முன் முத்தம் கல்யாணத்துக்கு வாறாக்களுக்கு. சுத்தி அப்பிடியே பின் வழியாப் போய் நிஹின்ஸாவைப் பார். (Hey where are you going? Front yard is for wedding guests. Go round the back and find Nihinsa.)

He turns and goes back the other way.

Has anyone seen my idiot husband?

A YOUNG WOMAN *enters, carrying a huge garland of flowers.*

If you damage those flowers I'll damage you! Stop giggling! This is a wedding, not a disco at the Blue Elephant!

YOUNG WOMAN: Yes Aacha!

The YOUNG WOMAN *exits, giggling uncontrollably.*

HASA *enters, rushing across the porch.*

AACHA: Hasa. Young man come here. / Hasa!

HASA: Aacha, I can't, my father's late and wants me to find a man / called—

AACHA: Hasa. Vinsanda can wait. Come here this minute!

HASA *walks back to* AACHA.

AACHA: Today, Hasa. You understand? The astrologer has looked over your star signs, he confirms that it's still a good match.

HASA: [*smiling*] Very good.

AACHA: He says the fourteenth of November, between eleven and two is auspicious—

HASA: So soon?

AACHA: We'll have the wedding here, of course—

HASA: But Aacha—

AACHA: Trust me Hasa. You are sure on your end, no?

HASA: Of course.

AACHA: Then leave my end up to me. But you must ask her today.

HASA: Yes, Aacha. Thank you. [*Beat*] I do have to go. My father is running late from Parliament—

AACHA: Apah is running late too—

HASA: He wants me to— the guests—

AACHA: Yes yes yes. Go.

He goes.

AACHA: Bloody Vinsanda, always getting in the way.

YOUNG THIRRU *enters, with a young woman,* SWATHI. *She wears simple clothes.*

Thirru! I didn't except to see you here?

YOUNG THIRRU: I came on the overnight bus, Aacha.

AACHA: Our house is being used for a wedding today. That minister's son is getting married to a Tamil girl and we're hosting the wedding here. As if we don't have enough politics in the house! Now— is Bala okay? Your mother?

YOUNG THIRRU: My family are safe, Aacha. இது என்ர தங்கச்சி ஸ்வாதி. (This is my younger sister, Swathi.)

SWATHI: வணக்கம் அன்ரி. (Hello, Aunty.)

YOUNG THIRRU: கொழும்புக்கு இது தான் முதல் தரம் இவவுக்கு (It's her first time in Colombo. In the city.)

AACHA: வா வா ஸ்வாதி. உங்கட அண்ணாவால எங்கள் எல்லாருக்கும் பெருமை. பழக்கடை வைச்சிருந்தவற்ற மகன் ஒரு எஞ்சினியர்! (Hello Swathi. Welcome. I'm so proud of your brother— [*pinching his cheeks*] The fruit seller's son is an engineer!)

The BANANA TREE MAN *enters.*

MALE SERVANT: ලොකු නෝනා, මෙන්න කෙසෙල් ගස් අරං ඇවිල්ලා (Loku nona, the banana tree man is here—)

AACHA: [*to* BANANA TREE MAN] எவ்வளவு நேரம் உனக்காகப் பாத்துக் கொண்டு நிக்கிறது? (Why are you so late?) [*To* MALE SERVANT] ඉස්සරහ ගේට්ටු කණුවල බඳින්න කියපං. මේ! හරියට ගාණට කෙළිං බැන්දේ නැත්තං මං සතයක් ගෙවන්නෑ! (Tell him to take the stems and tie them around the front gates, okay? And if they are not perfectly straight I will not pay him well!)

MALE SERVANT: හරි ලොකු නෝනා. (Yes, loku nona.)

The BANANA TREE MAN *puts up banana stalks. The* MALE SERVANT *watches.*

YOUNG THIRRU: Um, Aacha—

SUNIL *enters with a glass of whiskey.*

SUNIL: [*to* YOUNG THIRRU] Good day. [*To* AACHA] Good day.

He sits in Apah's chair.

What a wonderful home.

AACHA: Do I know you?

SUNIL: I don't believe so, no.

He extends a hand.

Sunil.

AACHA *doesn't take it. He withdraws his hand.*

I'm here on the invitation of the government. Diplomatic entourage from India! Today is my first day in Sri Lanka, actually. I'm impressed, far less dusty / than Madras—

AACHA: I don't care who you've been invited by, that's not your chair. Get up!

SUNIL *jumps out of the chair.*

This is my home, and when you are here, you will do what I say. Your politics don't carry any weight in my house. Got it?

SUNIL: Understood. It's a beautiful house, madam. I'm quite jealous!

YOUNG THIRRU: Aacha …

AACHA: Yes?

YOUNG THIRRU: ஸ்வாதி கொஞ்ச நாள் நிக்கலாமா? நான் நாளைக்கு யாழ்ப்பாணம் போகவேணும், ஆனா தங்கச்சி … (Would you mind if Swathi stayed here for a few days? I need to go back to Jaffna tomorrow, but my sister …)

AACHA: Yes?

YOUNG THIRRU: அவவுக்கு இங்க பாதுகாப்பு இருக்குமெண்டு நான் நினைக்கிறன். (I think she'd be safer here. For the time being.)

AACHA: I see.

A BRIDE *enters.*

BRIDE: Aacha!

AACHA: What is it *now* Manohari?

BRIDE: I think my hair piece fell off!

AACHA: *Moorooha!*

BRIDE: I *am* the bride you know.

AACHA: Go back to your dressing room. I'll be there in a moment.

BRIDE: [*exiting*] Aiyo! It's my wedding day you know, not your wedding day.

AACHA: Of course, Swathi can stay here for as long as she needs to. [*To* SWATHI] வா பிள்ளை. கல்யாணத்துக்கு இப்படி உடுத்துக்கொண்டு நிக்கேலாது.. என்ன சொல்றாய்? (Come darling, we can't have you looking like that at a wedding now can we?)

> AACHA *escorts* SWATHI *offstage.*

SWATHI: அண்ணா ... (Brother—)

YOUNG THIRRU: பறவாயில்ல தங்கச்சி ... போங்கோ. (It's okay little sister. Go.)

AACHA: Oh, and Thirru!

YOUNG THIRRU: Yes?

AACHA: Will you do *me* a favour?

YOUNG THIRRU: Of course.

AACHA: Stay here for me, and look out for my idiot husband. I told him, weddings are more important than politics. But does he listen? [*To* SUNIL] Why are you still here? Go and eat.

SUNIL: Of course madam, in a moment.

> AACHA *exits with* SWATHI.

Whiskey?

YOUNG THIRRU: No thank you.

> SUNIL *shrugs.*

SUNIL: So you know the people of this house?

YOUNG THIRRU: I do.

SUNIL: [*looking at his cheap clothes*] Obviously you are not part of the family.

YOUNG THIRRU: This house has been my home away from home.

SUNIL: I see.

YOUNG THIRRU: I'm from Jaffna. Thanks to Apah I was educated in Colombo. Now I'm an engineer.

SUNIL: A Jaffna boy, hey? Is that why you seem so ... uneasy?

> YOUNG THIRRU *turns his attention to* SUNIL.

Come now. How long has it been since the trouble up there? A few days or so?

YOUNG THIRRU: Two days.

SUNIL: Was your family caught up in it?

YOUNG THIRRU: Who are you?

ARIF enters with a lot of vattalapam (a Sri Lankan dessert).

ARIF: *Kolo! Vattalapam!*

The MALE SERVANT *and* NIHINSA *enter.*

NIHINSA: අරිෆ්! අනේ බොහොම ස්තුතියි. [*To male servant*] කොල්ලො, පරිස්සමිං අරං පලයං මේක ඇතුළට. වට්ටන්නෙ එහෙම නෑ හරිද? [*She mimes slapping him*] ඇහුණ නේද? (Arif! Thank you so much. Boy take that inside and don't drop it. Do you hear me?)

The MALE SERVANT *carefully and slowly exits with the trays of food.*

NIHINSA: Thirru—

YOUNG THIRRU: Nihinsa.

NIHINSA takes YOUNG THIRRU *to a private space.* SUNIL *sits down again in* APAH*'s chair.*

ඇයි මොකද? (What's wrong?) කියන්න (Tell me.)

NIHINSA: පොඩි මහත්තය ... මගේ මිනිහ අද උසාවි යනවා. (My husband goes into the courts today.)

YOUNG THIRRU: දකුණේ කලබල නින්දද ? (Because of the troubles down South?)

NIHINSA: එයා ගමේ වමේ කල්ලියක් එක්ක එකතුවෙලා. කතරගම පොලිසියට ගහද්දී එයත් ගිහින්. (He's quite taken up by this Marxist group in our village. He joined the attack on Katagarama police station.)

YOUNG THIRRU: ආ. (Ah.)

NIHINSA: එයා නිදහස් වෙයිද හිරේ යයිද කියලා අද තමයි දැනගන්නේ. (We find out today if he'll be set free, or given a sentence.)

YOUNG THIRRU: එහෙමද. (Yes.)

NIHINSA: මගුල්ගෙදර නින්දා මට යන්න බැරි උණා ... පොඩි පුතා ඇරියා. තව ටිකකින් උඹ එයි පණිවිඩේ අරන්. පොඩි

මහත්තයට පුලුවන්ද ... (I can't be there, because of this wedding. My younger son went instead. He'll come here soon, to tell me the decision. Could you—)

YOUNG THIRRU: මං හෝදිසියෙන් ඉන්නං. ආවම පැත්තකින් වාඩිකරවලා ඇවිත් නිහින්සට කියන්නම් (I'll look out for him. I'll make sure he sits quietly in the corner, then come and find you.)

NIHINSA *touches his face affectionately.*

NIHINSA: ලොකු උදව්වක්! එතකොට පොඩි මහත්තයගේ පවුලෙ අය? උතුරේ කලබල එක්ක ... ? (Thank you, thumbi. And you? With the troubles up North? Is your family okay?)

YOUNG THIRRU: දැනට හොඳින් ... (Yes. For now.)

The MALE SERVANT *has only just made it offstage when he drops everything.* NIHINSA *runs after him and chases him, screaming at him in Sinhala.*

YOUNG THIRRU *notices* SUNIL *watching him.*

SUNIL: You don't have to worry, Thirru. I'm separated from all that business. Cleeeeeeany separated. If anything, I'm here to help. We Indian and Sri Lankan Tamils must work together, no? இந்தியத் தமிழரும், இலங்கைத் தமிழரும் இணைந்து தான் செயற்படணும். அனுமான் என்ன தனியா வந்தார்ணு நினைக்கிறியா? (Didn't Hanuman travel from South India to Jaffna in one godly leap?) [*Extends his hand to* YOUNG THIRRU] My name is Sunil.

YOUNG THIRRU *does not take it.*

Is there a problem?

YOUNG THIRRU: Why must only 'Tamils' hold hands and walk together? 'Surely Tamils are not the only people in this country who believe in equality?'

SUNIL: Your words, or … ?

YOUNG THIRRU: Apah's.

SUNIL: They tell me that the famous 'Apah' no longer holds the influence he once did—

YOUNG RADHA *enters, brightly dressed. Following her is a* MIDDLE EASTERN MAN.

YOUNG RADHA: [*entering*] Whatever you are talking about, whoever you are—

> SUNIL *jumps out of the chair.*

—kindly leave my grandfather out of it.

SUNIL: You must be Radha.

YOUNG RADHA: Mister Mahadevan—yes?

SUNIL: Sunil Mahadevan.

YOUNG RADHA: Mister Mahadevan. This is Mister Levi. He has been searching high and low for you.

SUNIL: Mister Levi, my Israeli friend. Wonderful.

MISTER LEVI: It's a pleasure to meet you in person, Mister Mahadevan. I believe we have some business to conduct—

> AACHA *enters.*

AACHA: Any sign of Apah?

YOUNG THIRRU: Not yet Aacha.

> NIHINSA *enters.*

NIHINSA: ලොකු නෝන්නා ... පොඩ්ඩක් කතාකරන්න පුලුවන්ද? (Podi nona? Do you have a moment?)

AACHA: මොකද ළමයෝ? (What's it about, child?)

NIHINSA: පාර්ලිමේන්තුවෙන් පණිවිඩයක්! (A message from Parliament!)

> NIHINSA *whispers in* AACHA*'s ear.*

AACHA: That bloody Vinsanda!

> AACHA *exits into the house.* NIHINSA *follows her.*

SUNIL: *Interesting.*

YOUNG RADHA: Mister Mahadevan. All talk of a political or business matter is to be conducted in the VIP section, in the back yard. My grandmother has a rule about politics in our house.

> SUNIL *and* MISTER LEVI *look at* YOUNG RADHA.

Off you go!

> SUNIL *and* MISTER LEVI *exit.*

[*To* YOUNG THIRRU] Aacha says you brought Swathi with you?

YOUNG THIRRU: Hello, my mango-stealing friend!

YOUNG RADHA: Well did you?

YOUNG THIRRU: The slope of a vertical line is undefined. True or False?

YOUNG RADHA: Thirru! Is everything okay with your family in Jaffna?

YOUNG THIRRU: There are vector spaces that have infinite dimension. True or false?

YOUNG RADHA: Be serious!

YOUNG THIRRU: I got you!

YOUNG RADHA: No you didn't. Both your statements are true. *Obviously.*

YOUNG THIRRU: Okay then. So: Aacha says I brought Swathi with me …?

YOUNG RADHA: True.

YOUNG THIRRU: Everything is okay with my family in Jaffna … ?

YOUNG RADHA: True.

YOUNG THIRRU: *So don't worry.*

YOUNG RADHA: Why did you bring Swathi with you? How long are you staying here?

YOUNG THIRRU: What is the sum of one half, plus one quarter, plus one eighth, plus one sixteenth—

YOUNG RADHA: One night! You're staying one night?

> *The* MALE SERVANT *enters.*

MALE SERVANT: රාධා නෝන්නා (Radha—)

YOUNG RADHA: ඇයි ඇයි (What's wrong?)

MALE SERVANT: කවුද හරකෙක් අගමැතිතුමාගේ ඇඟේ වයින් හලලා! (Some idiot spilt wine on the Prime Minister—)

YOUNG RADHA: අයියෝ ... ඉතාලියෙන් ගෙන්නපු ඒවා (For goodness sake. It's foreign wine!) [*To* THIRRU] I'll be back.

> YOUNG RADHA *and the* MALE SERVANT *exit.*

> MAITHRI *enters, poorly dressed, clearly out of place.*

YOUNG THIRRU: නිහින්සගේ පුතාද? (Are you Nihinsa's son?)

> *The boy nods nervously.*

එන්න. මෙහෙන් වාඩිවෙන්න (Come. Sit.)

> YOUNG THIRRU *directs* MAITHRI *to the back.*

මෙතනම ඉන්න (Stay there.)

HASA *enters.*

HASA: Er— Have you seen Radha?

YOUNG THIRRU: I believe she is cleaning the Prime Minister.

HASA: Right. Right …

HASA *exits.* NIHINSA *enters.*

YOUNG THIRRU: Nihins—

A YOUNG WOMAN *rushes through with a collection of Hindu ceremonial items.* YOUNG THIRRU *and* NIHINSA *wait. The* YOUNG WOMAN *exits.*

NIHINSA *rushes to her son.*

NIHINSA: ඉක්මනට කියපං . ... මොකෝ නඩුකාරහාමුදුරුවෝ කිව්වේ? (Quickly. What did the judge say about my husband?)

MAITHRI *whispers in* NIHINSA*'s ear.*

Beat.

NIHINSA *takes* MAITHRI *by the ear, pinching hard.*

කාලකන්නියා ... මේක උඹේ වැරැද්ද! (Aday! Good for nothing rascal! This is your fault, you know!)

MAITHRI: ආයි ... අම්මේ! (Amma! Aiyo!)

NIHINSA: කියපන් ඉතින් ... දැන් මොකද කරන්නේ? (What are we going to do now? Eh?)

MAITHRI: ඒ කිව්වේ? (What do you mean?)

NIHNSA: ගිය සතියේ උඹට තිබුනා පැක්ටරිය අයිති මහත්තයා හම්බවෙන්න ... කෝ උඹ ගියාද? (Last week, you were supposed to go to the factory owner no? And did you?)

She lets go.

MAITHRI: අම්මේ එදා ලංකාව ඉන්දියාවට ගහලා ලෝක කුසලානේ ගත්තානේ! (That was the day of Sri Lanka's cricket world cup win over India!)

She grabs his ear again.

NIHINSA: එතකොට ඊයේ මම කිව්වා උඹට මාමව හම්බවෙලා උන්දැගේ හරක් බලාගන්න වැඩේ බාරගන්න කියලා? (And yesterday. You were supposed to meet Uncle about caring for his bullocks, no?)

MAITHRI: රජිනිකාන්ත් ගේ අලුත් පිච්චර් එක ආවා අම්මේ ... .
(But Rajinikanth's new movie came out—)

NIHINSA: වහපිය කට! (Shut up!) [*Beat*] උඹේ නංගී, ආච්චි
අම්මලා සීයලා ... උන් බඩගින්නේ ... උන්ටත් එක්ක කන්න
අදින්න හොයන්න ඕනේ. (We must eat, no? Your sister, your
grandparents—we will have to take care of them now too—they
must all eat, no?)

MAITHRI: [*head bowed*] ඔව් අම්මේ (Yes.)

>   AACHA's *voice is heard from offstage.*

AACHA: [*offstage*] Nihinsa!

NIHINSA: [*to* MAITHRI] ඔතනින් වාඩිවෙයං ... හෙල්ලෙන් නෑ!
(Sit over there … And don't move!)

MAITHRI: හා. (Okay.)

>   MAITHRI *sits at the back.*

>   AACHA *enters.*

AACHA: I have to attend to a problem. The banana tree man and his
cronies? උන්ටත් හරියට කන්න හම්බුනාද කියලා බලන්න
නිහින්සා. (Make sure they are all fed well.)

NIHINSA: හොඳයි ලොකු නෝන්නා. (Yes, loku nona.)

AACHA: අර තඩි මනුස්සයා ඉන්නේ ... සෆාරි සූට් එකක්
ඇඳන් ... එයා තමයි අලුත් වෙළඳ ඇමති. එයාට තව
විස්කි ඇල්ලුවනම් හොඳයි. එයාට එහාපැත්තෙ ඉන්න
තැම්බිච්ච ඉස්සෙක් වගේ මනුස්සයා බ්‍රිතාන්‍ය ඛනිජ තෙල්
සංස්ථාවෙන් . ... එයාට තව වතුර ඇල්ලුවනම් හොඳයි. (You
see the very large fellow in the safari suit. That's the new Trade
Minister. He needs to drink more whiskey. The sunburnt white
man beside him is from British Petroleum. He needs to drink more
water.)

NIHINSA: හොඳයි ලොකු නෝන්නා (Yes, loku nona.)

>   AACHA *exits.*

[*To* MAITHRI] උඹ හෙල්ලෙනවා නෙවෙයි ඔතනින්! (Don't
move. Idiot!)

>   NIHINSA *exits.* YOUNG RADHA *enters.*

YOUNG RADHA: Nothing a bit of vinegar can't fix. Did my grandmother
go this way?

She goes to exit.

YOUNG THIRRU: [*stopping her*] I have something for you.

> YOUNG THIRRU *gives* YOUNG RADHA *a piece of paper covered in handwritten numbers.*

YOUNG RADHA: What is this?

YOUNG THIRRU: It's … um … a mathematical joke. I wrote it on the bus.

> YOUNG RADHA *reads it and laughs.*

YOUNG THIRRU: You like it?

YOUNG RADHA: Actually, there's an error.

YOUNG THIRRU: Oh.

YOUNG RADHA: But it's still funny! See here— / or even better …

YOUNG THIRRU: Of course …

> *She takes a pencil from his top pocket and begins to re-write the equation.*

YOUNG RADHA: Aacha said your sister came with you.

YOUNG THIRRU: One of her friends was killed in the troubles. A couple of days ago.

YOUNG RADHA: Oh no. I'm so sorry, Thirru.

YOUNG THIRRU: She's quite upset.

YOUNG RADHA: Of course.

YOUNG THIRRU: Upset and angry.

YOUNG RADHA: I see.

YOUNG THIRRU: இளம் ஆக்கள் கோவப்படுறதுக்கு இது நல்ல நேரமில்லை. இயக்கங்கள் எல்லாம் ஆள் சேர்த்துக் கொண்டிருக்குது. (It is not a good time to be young and angry.)

> *He looks around to make sure no-one is listening.*

There are groups that take advantage of such people …

YOUNG RADHA: [*softly*] விடுதலைப் புலிகள் (The Tigers.)

YOUNG THIRRU: She would like to join them Radha. I can't let her join them. So I have brought her here for a few days and we will go back North when things are quieter and probably then … I will have to stay in Jaffna.

> *Beat.*

YOUNG RADHA: You're moving back to Jaffna?

> AACHA *enters,* NIHINSA *following.* YOUNG THIRRU *and* YOUNG RADHA *step apart.*

AACHA: Radha. Darling, your pleats aren't straight!

> AACHA *pulls a pin out of her blouse to fasten the pleats.*

YOUNG RADHA: Aacha! Don't worry about these things!

AACHA: Nonsense. It is very important that you look absolutely perfect today.

YOUNG RADHA: I'm not the one getting married.

AACHA: Why not? You are twenty-two already! [*To* YOUNG THIRRU] Ridiculous that she is not married already, no?

YOUNG THIRRU: [*cheeky*] Ridiculous.

AACHA: Her own parents are running around Canada and Australia selling cinnamon to *vellakaran*. Only me to worry about her. Twenty-two and still not married! Thirru, do me a favour. Take your engineering degree and look at the swing for the wedding. The bride is worried it won't be able to bear the weight of her future husband.

YOUNG RADHA: I don't think the groom is the problem.

> YOUNG RADHA *and* YOUNG THIRRU *crack up.*

AACHA: Stupid children! Thirru go and fix the swing! I don't want it to collapse in the middle of the ceremony.

YOUNG RADHA: I don't think there's anything you can do. It's going to collapse no matter what. Too many *laddus* have been eaten.

> *More giggling from both the youngsters.*

AACHA: Stop it! Thirru, go now!

YOUNG THIRRU: You don't want me to keep a look out for Apah?

AACHA: Apah is in prison.

YOUNG RADHA: What! Why?

AACHA: The usual reasons. For being troublesome and pig-headed. [*Beat.*] Not to worry, I have taken care of it. Weddings are more important than Parliament. Thirru, please fix the swing for the fat couple.

YOUNG THIRRU: Absolutely, Aacha.

YOUNG THIRRU *exits.* AACHA *finishes fixing* YOUNG RADHA's *saree.*

YOUNG RADHA: Why is / Apah in—

AACHA: You know, it wouldn't surprise me one bit if the groom had already got that woman pregnant.

YOUNG RADHA: Aacha!

AACHA: [*turning* YOUNG RADHA *in her saree*] This *palu* is lovely, no?

YOUNG RADHA: I told the bride when I'm married I want to have a son and call him Siddhartha. [*Beat.*] She only smiled also.

AACHA: Radha, you can give your child a Sinhala name, that's perfectly fine. *My* business—the *first* order of business—is *whom* you marry. The name can come later. Hasa is going to be a brilliant match for you.

YOUNG RADHA: Not again!

AACHA: The *ayar* says it's auspicious—

YOUNG RADHA: How would he know? Did you go to the *ayar* without asking me?

AACHA: Why shouldn't I?

YOUNG RADHA: I told you, I'm not ready to get married.

AACHA: You think a marriage is just two people. Rubbish. Look around. Do you even see the bride and groom? Nothing but families. In your case both families are in high agreement.

YOUNG RADHA: Well he hasn't asked me yet anyway.

AACHA: That's a small and temporary issue.

YOUNG RADHA: I'm not going to talk about this.

AACHA: I've done all the preparatory work Radha. All you have to do is realise that you're as obstinate as your grandfather and agree to the match.

YOUNG RADHA: I don't love Hasa.

AACHA: I didn't love your Apah.

YOUNG RADHA: You didn't?

AACHA: I could tell he had a serious intellect. I knew he was a responsible man. And he had quite a sexy bum!

YOUNG RADHA: Aacha!

AACHA: But now I love the rascal deeply. We have taken care of each other.

The HOPPER MAN *enters again.*

YOUNG RADHA *and* AACHA: You have to go around the back! Ask for Nihinsa.

He turns and goes back the way he came again.

AACHA: Do you understand, darling? [*Beat.*] The answer is, yes, Aacha.

YOUNG RADHA *bows her head.*

YOUNG RADHA: Yes, Aacha.

HASA *enters, whiskey in hand.*

AACHA: Hasa! Splendid timing.
HASA: Hello, Radha.
YOUNG RADHA: Hello, Hasa.
AACHA: Come.
HASA: My father's running late, I should—

He goes to leave.

AACHA: Hasa. Come here!
HASA: Yes Aacha.
AACHA: Could you take Radha to the gate to tie up the banana stalks?
YOUNG RADHA: They're already up.
AACHA: Not properly.
YOUNG RADHA: They are very tall and straight.
AACHA: Radha!

She takes HASA*'s whiskey.*

Give me that.

She tips it out.

[*To both of them*:] Go on.

HASA *and* YOUNG RADHA *exit.*

AACHA: [*under her breath*] Bloody hard work.

YOUNG THIRRU *enters.*

YOUNG THIRRU: That swing is now strong enough to hold an elephant.
AACHA: Thirru I'm very proud of you. Your parents must be extremely proud of you. You can fix a swing, you can build a bridge. Come, Thirru, look.

She points offstage, to where HASA *took* YOUNG RADHA.

AACHA: See how sweetly they walk together? Like a movie, no?

YOUNG THIRRU: Who, Hasa and Radha?

AACHA: Both families are in approval of the match. We are going to have the wedding right here, in a few months.

YOUNG THIRRU: Oh.

AACHA: So exciting, no?

> AACHA *squeezes* YOUNG THIRRU'*s hand in excitement and exits.*
>
> YOUNG THIRRU *watches.*
>
> *He turns and sits down.*
>
> *He folds his mathematical joke and puts it back in his pocket.*
>
> NIHINSA *rushes across the stage.*

NIHINSA: ලොකු නෝනාව දැක්කද? හදිසියක් ... (Have you seen Aacha? I need to find her ...)

YOUNG THIRRU: What's the matter—

NIHINSA: ගේ ඇතුලෙ, පොලිටික්ස්! (Politics in the house!)

> *She has already exited.*
>
> *A commotion.* APAH, *handcuffed to a chair, is being carried through the audience by two* POLICEMAN. VINSANDA *follows.*
>
> *The noise brings others onto the porch, including* YOUNG RADHA *and* HASA.

VINSANDA: We are talking about violent, anarchist thugs, Apah! They are *dangerous*. We have to be able to extinguish that danger swiftly and efficiently.

YOUNG THIRRU: [*calling out*] Aacha!

> YOUNG THIRRU *exits.*

APAH: I will admit one thing Vinsanda: you do not discriminate. Whether it be the Sinhala Marxist insurgents down South or the Tamil boys up North, you seem equally happy to execute them all!

VINSANDA: We only execute the extremely violent—the rest are given imprisonment, according to the law.

> *The entourage arrives on stage.*

Radha, darling! I don't see you as much these days—

YOUNG RADHA: Apah, what on earth is going on? Are you okay?

The POLICEMEN *set* APAH *down and collapse.*

APAH: Everything is perfectly fine, darling. Although I must admit I am rather *hungry*.

VINSANDA: I can't account for his dignity, but physically at least he is suitably intact.

APAH: Have they served the main meals yet?

YOUNG RADHA: You must *both* tell me what is *going on*—

SUNIL *and* MISTER LEVI *enter.*

VINSANDA: Ah! Our guests from the international delegation!

APAH: Who invited those low lives?

VINSANDA: I did, Apah.

APAH: You rascal. Into my house?

VINSANDA: You decided to pull this stunt of yours on the most annoying day possible—

APAH: You invited that upon yourself—

VINSANDA: —and so I invited these two upon *you*.

SWATHI *enters and hurries to* YOUNG RADHA.

YOUNG RADHA:ஸ்வாதி ... ஹல்லோ.திருசொன்னவர் ... (Swathi, hello. Thirru told me about you—)

She gives YOUNG RADHA *a note.*

SWATHI: ராதா ... இது என்ர அண்ணாவுக்கு. (Please. Radha. For my brother.) Tell him ... tell him that I will do what he cannot.

SWATHI *quickly exits through the audience.*

YOUNG RADHA: Swathi!

SUNIL: Vinsanda! Good to see you again. And Mister Mannikavasar. The famous Apah!

VINSANDA: Mister Levi! Mister Mahadevan! [*He shakes their hands*] I'm sorry Apah can't shake your hand, he's somewhat occupied at the moment—

APAH: I'm fully aware of why you are in Sri Lanka, Mister Mahadevan. I would not care to shake your hand even if I were free to do so.

SUNIL: It must run in the family.

NIHINSA *enters with* AACHA.

AACHA: Gentleman, dinner is being served.

APAH: *Splendid*. Vinsanda, order your men to take these bloody things off—

VINSANDA: I shall do no such thing.

APAH: Excuse me?

VINSANDA: Technically you are still under arrest.

AACHA: Vinsanda!

> *Beat.*

VINSANDA: [*to the* POLICEMAN] එක මාංචුවක් ගලවන්න! (You may undo one set of handcuffs!)

> YOUNG THIRRU *enters.*

YOUNG THIRRU: [*to* AACHA] Ah! You found him.

AACHA: Radha, did your grandfather tell you about the silly nonsense he got up to today?

YOUNG RADHA: Not yet. [*To* YOUNG THIRRU] Thirru, Swathi was here—

YOUNG THIRRU: Yes?

YOUNG RADHA: She left—

YOUNG THIRRU: What? Where to?

AACHA: And did Vinsanda Mama tell you about the silly nonsense he got up to today?

YOUNG RADHA: No—

HASA: [*to* YOUNG THIRRU] She went that way—

> YOUNG THIRRU *exits.*

YOUNG RADHA: Thirru …

> *She is still holding the note Swathi gave her.*

AACHA: Radha! Vinsanda Uncle put your Apah in prison today.

HASA: What? [*To* VINSANDA] *You* put Apah in prison?

YOUNG RADHA: [*to* VINSANDA] *You* did this?

AACHA: I have enough to do today. Must I also organise my rascal husband's release?

YOUNG RADHA: Apah! Is this true?

APAH: Nihinsa, prepare a meal for me inside? Today is not the best day for me to fraternise with our guests.

NIHINSA: හොදයි ලොකු මහත්තයා (Yes, Apah.)

> *She exits.*

YOUNG RADHA: Once and for all, would somebody please tell me what has been going on!

APAH: No need to get so excited darling. Just relax. Stop and think. Where to begin?

> *Beat. A large group of people have gathered to watch.*

YOUNG RADHA: Why are you handcuffed to this chair?

APAH: I am *protesting*, darling.

YOUNG RADHA: Of course. But what are you protesting *today*?

APAH: This country's slide from democracy into dictatorship.

BYSTANDER 1: / ஓம் அப்பா, ஓமப்பா! (Yes Apah, yes Apah!)

BYSTANDER 2: What nonsense.

VINSANDA: What stupendous nonsense! We won a fair election.

APAH: And then you neutered the opposition. Tens of thousands of Sinhala villagers were driven from their homes in the South.

VINSANDA: They were violent. Order must come first.

BYSTANDER 3: Order for who?

VINSANDA: For this country!

AACHA: Must you have a shouting match in front of all our guests?

> NIHINSA *enters.*

NIHINSA: ලොකු නෝනා සමාවෙන්න බාදා කරාට ... කෑම අරින්න වෙලාව හරි (Loku nona, sorry to interrupt, it's time to serve the meals—)

AACHA: හරි හරි හරි. වෙලාව හරි (Yes yes yes. Fine.) [*To* APAH *and* VINSANDA] I'm not finished with you. Either of you.

> AACHA *and* NIHINSA *exit.* YOUNG RADHA *watches* NIHINSA *go.*

YOUNG RADHA: Nihinsa's family were run out of Elpitiya. That's their ancestral village. They lost everything.

VINSANDA: Nihinsa's husband is a militant Marxist. He was part of the attack on the Kataragama police station.

APAH: Today he was given twelve years' imprisonment—

YOUNG RADHA: My God—

APAH: Twenty years ago Nihinsa was energised about politics. Now she has given up on our leaders.

MISTER LEVI: [*to* VINSANDA] Hold on. Just to clarify— you now have no opposition at *all*?

VINSANDA: Of course there is an opposition. But they don't stand for their country.

BYSTANDER 2: Only for themselves.

> YOUNG THIRRU *enters.*

YOUNG RADHA: All of the Tamil parties merged into the Tamil United Liberation Front. The T.U.L.F. won every single Tamil-speaking seat. They are the new opposition.

MISTER LEVI: And you, Apah— I assume you are part of this T.U.L.F.?

APAH: Certainly not.

VINSANDA: Apah is a party of one.

APAH: What do you say, Radha?

YOUNG RADHA: The T.U.L.F. campaigned for a separate country up North for Tamils—Tamil Eelam. This is not who we are. Sri Lanka is one country with many castes and creeds within it.

BYSTANDER 1: துரோகி! துரோகி! (Traitor! Traitor!)

APAH: Well said, darling!

> NIHINSA *enters.*

VINSANDA: No surprises there. The granddaughter always parrots her grandfather. Party of two.

HASA: I agree with Radha. Sorry Father.

VINSANDA: My own son. Party of three! Apah I've found some young followers to feebly continue your dwindling legacy.

YOUNG RADHA: I would be proud to! Everyone is so busy forming their own united fronts that the country itself is united about precisely nothing.

SUNIL: Thirru. Tell us, what do *you* think of the United National Party being back in government?

> *Everyone turns to look at him.*

YOUNG THIRRU: I …

APAH: Speak, Thirru!

> *Beat.*

YOUNG THIRRU: It doesn't matter who's in government.

APAH: Excuse me?

YOUNG THIRRU: No-one will protect us.

YOUNG RADHA: Thirru?

> *Beat. Everyone is still looking at him.*

YOUNG THIRRU: Two days ago in Jaffna my sister and I were at a school carnival. A group of police arrived drunk. All the police are Sinhala. When they were asked to pay like everyone else they physically attacked the organisers. Members of the public attacked them back—

VINSANDA: A stupid move—

YOUNG THIRRU: —so the police opened fire on the crowd.

VINSANDA: A policeman was killed—

BYSTANDER 1: Four of our people were killed!

YOUNG THIRRU: Including my sister's friend. Then the gossip spread that Tamils had attacked Sinhala policemen—

> *Overlapping:*

BYSTANDER 2: People said Tamils attacked Buddhist temples and Sinhala shops—

BYSTANDER 3: They did.

BYSTANDER 1: No! My brother was there! They did no such thing!

YOUNG THIRRU: Soon there was mass violence across the North. But where was the government? Where was the government?

VINSANDA: 'Mass violence' is a rather extreme way to describe it.

HASA: What would you know, father?

> *Beat.*

VINSANDA: Excuse me?

HASA: Have you ever been in a riot?

VINSANDA: I've been stopping riots for longer than you've been alive, child.

HASA: Yesterday I was reporting down South, near Aluthgama. A pregnant Tamil woman was chased into a sugar cane field. The mobs set the field alight, they caught the woman and ripped open her / belly—

BYSTANDER 3: / Oh my God.

VINSANDA: / Hasa, this is a wedding—

YOUNG THIRRU: Tens of thousands of Tamils in the middle of the country have been driven out of their homes. They have all had to flee up North.

YOUNG RADHA: In a few weeks of your election fifty thousand people have become refugees in their own country—

BYSTANDER 1: My cousin has sold his shop. We don't feel welcome in the South anymore.

YOUNG RADHA: Violence has become normal for you. It's just another political tool—

VINSANDA: We've arrested the perpetrators. That is our job.

APAH: Oh yes, your government loves arresting people.

YOUNG THIRRU: But no-one can actually keep us safe. Isn't that the first duty of those we elect?

NIHINSA: [*pointing at* YOUNG THIRRU] ඒක තමයි ඇත්ත (That is the truth.)

> *Everyone looks at her. Pause.*

VINSANDA: [*angered, to* YOUNG THIRRU] If you really want the riots to stop, Thirru, talk to your own leaders. The T.U.L.F. say they want a separate state! They say they do not use violence, but they *suggest* violence may come in the future. How do you expect the majority to react?

BYSTANDER 2: We live in fear.

YOUNG THIRRU: The T.U.L.F. are not our leaders. They hold rallies in the villages. They tell us to be proud of being Tamil. Of speaking Tamil. But they pay for private tutors to teach their own children Sinhala, so they can land government jobs in Colombo. [*Beat.*] The young ones in Jaffna like my sister have given up on the Tamil leadership. They watch Sinhala police shoot their friends in schoolyards. They trust no-one. And now … Now the real problem is, they have decided to take matters into their own hands.

MISTER LEVI: Forgive me, but I don't see how all this leads to you being handcuffed to this chair.

APAH: Good point, thank you. Today the U.N.P. tabled a new bill—

VINSANDA: In response to politically motivated violence that is putting the majority population in danger—

APAH: An 'anti-terrorism' bill in which they seek the right to imprison and execute people—

VINSANDA: Only those terrorists who are considered a danger to the state—

APAH: —without proper judicial or parliamentary review.

YOUNG RADHA: That is outrageous!

APAH: Your Apah has limited power to change policy these days, Radha. But even a party of one has tactics.

VINSANDA: What— to act like a bullish child?

APAH: I simply talked in Parliament for four hours straight and there was no time for anyone to pass any bill of any kind.

YOUNG RADHA: That sounds like an intelligent tactic to me.

VINSANDA: *Simply* talked for four hours and simply refused to vacate his chair when the speaker ordered him to, so security picked him up where he sat and carried him out, *still talking.*

The BYSTANDERS *laugh.*

They put him down on Galle Road. Hundreds gathered around him as they sat in the sun in protest. He went on bloody talking so I told the police to simply pick him up and carry him to prison where he can bloody well talk as much as he likes without causing public disturbances and legislative chaos.

YOUNG RADHA: Apah. You are too old for this.

APAH: I cannot be silent, Radha.

VINSANDA: We'll pass the policy tomorrow. If not then, the day after. And if not then, the day after that.

An uncomfortable pause.

YOUNG RADHA: [*to the* POLICEMAN] තව මාංචුවක් තියෙනවද?
(Do you have another pair of handcuffs?)

POLICEMAN: Yes ma'am.

YOUNG RADHA: Give them to me.

VINSANDA: Don't give / them to her!

He does.

YOUNG RADHA: Thank you Sir.

YOUNG RADHA *handcuffs herself to the chair. A gasp from everyone.*

APAH: Radha, what are you doing?

YOUNG RADHA: Vinsanda Mama, I will not marry your son.

APAH: / What?

VINSANDA: I beg your pardon?

YOUNG RADHA: His opinions I like. I like him. But I will not marry for alliance. Not for class. Not for the sake of trying to rescue an old friendship that is being destroyed by politics—

APAH: Radha—

YOUNG RADHA: And I certainly cannot marry into the family of a man whose government is determined to drag Sri Lanka into madness and horror.

APAH: Radha this is not the occasion—

YOUNG RADHA: Tell that to Vinsanda! Tell that to yourself! Crashing in here like a pair of golden elephants.

     AACHA *enters.*

YOUNG RADHA: Weddings are more important than politics! Aren't they Aacha?

AACHA: What on earth is going on? [*To* VINSANDA] Did you do this?

VINSANDA: Radha did it to herself.

YOUNG RADHA: This is my protest. All of Sri Lanka has been hijacked by politics. Schools, shops, hospitals, houses, now even weddings. People must live! Life must hijack politics!

AACHA: What is going on?

MISTER LEVI: This Radha girl is not going to marry this Hasa fellow.

AACHA: Who are you? What?

YOUNG RADHA: I'm not going to marry into that man's family.

AACHA: You will do what your elders tell you.

YOUNG RADHA: Look what our elders have done to Sri Lanka!

AACHA: [*advancing on* YOUNG RADHA] How dare you—

YOUNG RADHA: But Aacha—

     AACHA *slaps* YOUNG RADHA. *Another gasp from the onlookers.*

AACHA: You think you know everything? You think life is just about shouting out whatever thoughts come into your bloody head?

APAH: Aacha. Leave her be. It's okay.

AACHA: It is certainly not okay. Now tell me. What is going on?

VINSANDA: Hasanga?

HASA: Radha and I have talked. She's in love with someone else.

AACHA: Who? Who are you in love with?

YOUNG RADHA: I'm not telling.

AACHA: [*to* HASA] Who is she in love with?

HASA: Isn't it obvious?

AACHA: No it isn't bloody obvious!

APAH: Radha why did you chain yourself to my chair?

YOUNG RADHA: [*laughing at herself*] I don't know. To change the game! No more politics! Only life!

AACHA: Stupid girl, shut up and tell us who it is?

BYSTANDER 3: Who does she love?

YOUNG RADHA: I'm not telling.

APAH: Radha, darling, it's not a protest until you know your demands.

YOUNG RADHA: Okay. [*Beat*] Weddings are more important than politics. Vinsanda Mama, say it.

VINSANDA: Radha …

YOUNG RADHA: Weddings are more important than politics!

VINSANDA: You know that isn't true—

YOUNG RADHA: It is true! We must live life first!

VINSANDA: There is no life to live without politics.

AACHA: Just shut up and say it, man!

> *Beat.*

VINSANDA: Weddings are more important than politics.

YOUNG RADHA: Second. [*Thinks, then:*] Women run their families better than you run the country.

VINSANDA: This is very silly.

YOUNG RADHA: Women run their families better than you run the country.

VINSANDA: Oh my God.

YOUNG RADHA: Say it. Apah. Say it.

APAH: Women run their families better than we run the country.

YOUNG RADHA: Vinsanda Mama.

VINSANDA: Women run their families better than we run the country.

YOUNG RADHA: And third—I can marry who I choose.

APAH: I trust you to pick the right person, Radha.

YOUNG RADHA: Aacha?

> *Beat.*

AACHA: Who are you in love with?

YOUNG RADHA: I can marry who I choose.

Pause.

AÁCHA: Marry whoever you bloody like just stop torturing me. Who? Who?

Beat. YOUNG RADHA *looks at* YOUNG THIRRU. *Everyone looks at* YOUNG THIRRU.

YOUNG THIRRU: Me?

Pause.

AACHA: I should have known. [*To* APAH] This is your fault. The pair of you, fix it up now. Lunch is waiting!

APAH: Radha. Any more demands?

YOUNG RADHA *is looking at* YOUNG THIRRU.

YOUNG RADHA: … No.

APAH: Then unlock yourself from my chair.

The POLICEMAN *unlocks her.*

[*To* VINSANDA] So? What now?

VINSANDA: Hasa?

HASA: Of course.

VINSANDA: Okay.

APAH: Very good.

VINSANDA: Very good.

APAH: Aacha?

She looks at YOUNG RADHA. YOUNG RADHA *is looking at* YOUNG THIRRU.

AACHA: Okay fine. For now. [*To* VINSANDA] Unlock my husband.

VINSANDA *nods to the* POLICEMAN.

[*To* VINSANDA] I won't tell you again. No. Politics. In. My. House.

VINSANDA *offers his hand to* APAH.

VINSANDA: It's just cricket, my friend.

Beat.

APAH: See you back at the crease tomorrow, Vinsanda.

They shake hands.

AACHA: Go and eat. Everybody. I'm fed up with the lot of you.

The fragile little society assembled disperses to eat.

[*To* HASA] Go and have some whiskey. And pour me a brandy from my cupboard.

HASA: Yes Aacha.

HASA *exits.*

YOUNG THIRRU: Radha—

AACHA: No. I'm not finished with you two. Radha take your grandfather inside. Nihinsa put a plate of food in his study.

YOUNG RADHA: How did you get Apah out of prison?

AACHA: The groom is the son of the Minster of Justice. Go. Inside.

YOUNG RADHA: Yes, Aacha. [*To* YOUNG THIRRU] Swathi gave me this, it's for you.

APAH *and* YOUNG RADHA *exit.*

YOUNG THIRRU *opens the note. He reads it, then runs off stage, the same way* SWATHI *exited.* AACHA *watches him go:*

AACHA: The fruit seller's son thinks he can marry my daughter. Not while I am still breathing.

NIHINSA *stands and looks out across the wedding.* AACHA *walks to her.*

අවුරුදු 12ක හිර දඬුවමක්? (They gave your husband twelve years?)

NIHINSA: ඔව් ලොකු නෝන්නා (Yes, loku nona.)

AACHA *gives her some money.*

AACHA: ළමයින්ගෙ වියදංවලට (For the children.)

NIHINSA: පිං ලොකු නෝන්නා (Thank you, loku nona.)

NIHINSA *takes it and tucks it into her saree. She looks at* MAITHRI.

අපේ එක්කෙනා පවුල අමතක කරලා දේශපාලනේ කරන්න ගියා. මගේ ලොකු එකා කමකට නැති නිකමෙක්. උගෙ නං කවුරුත් කසාද බඳින එකක් නෑ (My husband chose his politics over his family. My son is useless. No-one will marry him.)

AACHA: උඹේ හිතහැදෙන්න මොනවා කියන්නද කියලා මට

හිතාගන්න බෑ නිහින්සා (I'd be lying if I said I had any answers, Nihinsa.)

AACHA *exits.*

NIHINSA *pulls* MAITHRI *up by the ear.*

NIHINSA: කොල්ලො උඹ හමුදාවට බැදියන් (Boy. You must join the army.)

MAITHRI: මොනවා? (What?)

NIHINSA: හමුදාවෙදි වගේ දෙගුණයක් ජීවිත මහපාරේ අනතුරැ වලින් නැතිවෙනවයි කියන්නේ! මේ කාලේ, එහෙම ස්ථීර රස්සාවක් හොයාගන්න වෙන්නෑ. උඹ මං වගේ මෙහෙකාරකං කරනවා දකින්න මට බෑ. උඹ හමුදාවට බැදෙන්න ඕනේ (Just as many people lose their lives each year in traffic accidents as get killed in the army. It's the most stable job in the country right now. Radha can demand her rights but we can't demand ours. We must break out of this. You must join the army.)

MAITHRI *bows his head.*

මට තව වැඩ තියෙනවා. (I have to work.)

She gives him the money.

Buy dinner for your sister. Go!

NIHINSA *and* MAITHRI *exit in different directions.* YOUNG THIRRU *enters. He is alone.*

YOUNG RADHA *enters.*

They look at each other.

RADHA *stands up.*

YOUNG THIRRU: I don't know if today is the happiest or the saddest day of my life.

He holds up the note from SWATHI.

Swathi has gone to join the Tigers. You don't want our troubles in your life, Radha. You shouldn't marry me.

Beat.

Radha?

SIDDHARTHA *and* LILY *enter.*

SCENE FOUR

SIDDHARTHA: [*to* RADHA] Amma?

Sydney, 2004.

Amma, this is my … This is Lily. I know this is a shock for you but you've barely said anything for weeks and this is just how it is now. I'm sorry. I think Thirru's going to call tonight. I got a text message from plus-six zero one six—that's Malaysia. 'Your father safe. Wait please.' That's from Malaysia.

RADHA *looks at* LILY.

LILY: Hi, Radha Aunty. I've heard a lot about you, it's nice to finally—

RADHA *exits.*

I thought that went well.

SWATHI *enters.*

MAITHRI *enters, dressed in army uniform and with a gun.*

A TAMIL TIGERS OFFICER *enters. He carries a Liberation Tigers of Tamil Eelam (LTTE) uniform.* SWATHI *runs to him. He says an LTTE battle cry and she repeats it. She takes the uniform and they exit.*

NIHINSA *enters.* MAITHRI *walks to her. She holds his face affectionately and offers a Buddhist prayer before pushing him away. They exit.*

RADHA *enters, carrying a cup of tea. She offers it to* LILY, *gives her a kiss on the forehead.* SIDDHARTHA *takes* LILY*'s hand. They gather around the phone.*

SIDDHARTHA: Now we wait.

A PEOPLE SMUGGLER *hurries through with two or three* ASYLUM SEEKERS. *One of them is* THIRRU.

THIRRU *gives the* SMUGGLER *cash. He mimes the act of a phone. The* PEOPLE SMUGGLER *shakes his head.* THIRRU *gives him the gold chain around his neck, and mimes again. The* SMUGGLER *gives him a phone, and a calling card.*

SMUGGLER: Hurry.

>THIRRU *dials a long number.*

>*The phone in Radha's living room rings.* SIDDHARTHA *answers.*

SIDDHARTHA: Hello?

THIRRU: Siddhartha?

SIDDHARTHA: Thirru?

THIRRU: Hello. / Can you hear me?

SIDDHARTHA: I can hear you. Can you hear me?

THIRRU: Hello? Siddhartha, / I'm sorry—

SIDDHARTHA: I'm putting you on speakerphone. Can you hear me?

THIRRU: Hello Siddhartha?

SIDDHARTHA: Where are you? / I'm here with Amma and my—

THIRRU: I don't know exactly where—

SIDDHARTHA: And Lily. My girlfriend Lily.

THIRRU: Your *what*?

>*Beat.*

SIDDHARTHA: We're in a relationship.

LILY: Hello Thirru.

>*Beat.*

THIRRU: I hope to meet you one day, Lily.

LILY: I hope so too, Thirru.

SIDDHARTHA: Where have you been? / I got a text from—

THIRRU: / I'm in Indonesia.

SIDDHARTHA: / —from Malaysia.

THIRRU: No no, Indonesia.

SIDDHARTHA: Sorry?

THIRRU: Somewhere in Indonesia. / I'm about to get on a boat.

SIDDHARTHA: I got a text from plus-six zero one six. Malaysia.

LILY: [*to* SIDDHARTHA] Siddhartha …

THIRRU: Radha?

SIDDHARTHA: No, Amma's not— Why are you in Indonesia?

>*The* PEOPLE SMUGGLER *hurries through again with two or three more* ASYLUM SEEKERS.

SIDDHARTHA: You were in India right?

As the SMUGGLER *passes* THIRRU *he motions to him.*

SMUGGLER: Hurry!

THIRRU: Siddhartha I'm getting on a boat.

SIDDHARTHA: What boat?

THIRRU: I *was* in Malaysia. But I couldn't call you, I'm sorry Siddhartha. I was locked in a room—

SIDDHARTHA: How did you end up in Malaysia?

THIRRU: First I was in Rameshwaram. / No, first I was in Mannar—

SIDDHARTHA: Rameshwaram— that's / India right?

THIRRU: In Colombo Sunil put me on a truck to Mannar. A man in Mannar put me on a boat to Rameshwaram. In Rameshwaram I registered as a refugee. There were families there who had been registered there for thirty-four years Siddhartha, I met a man who was born and grew / up there—

The SMUGGLER *runs through with more* ASYLUM SEEKERS.

SIDDHARTHA: Thirru what's going on? We didn't hear from you in weeks and now / you're in—

THIRRU: In Rameshwaram a man from Sunil gives me a false passport with visa to Malaysia. But in Kuala Lumpur the smugglers locked me in a room. I was locked in a room with maybe thirty other people, I'm sorry, Siddhartha, there were no phones, no clocks / and I don't know how long—

SIDDHARTHA: / Thirru?

THIRRU: I got very sick. Everyone was sick. After I don't know how long a man appears and says tomorrow the Malaysian police will come and they will take the Tamils and give them back to the Sri Lankan Government—but if you pay you can leave tonight. So I give this man all my money and we leave and today we are in Indonesia and I'm sorry Siddhartha, we are taking a boat. We are taking a boat tonight. I have learnt the words.

SIDDHARTHA: Appa? What boat? What boat Appa?!

THIRRU: I'm getting on a boat to become a refugee in Australia.

SIDDHARTHA: Do *not* get on that boat! People die on those boats!

THIRRU: They will send me back to Sri Lanka! They will lock me in a room! They will put me in a camp for thirty-four years! I will die as a refugee, Siddhartha! I have to take the boat.

The SMUGGLER *runs through with more* ASYLUM SEEKERS.

SMUGGLER: Come! Now!

SIDDHARTHA: You can catch a plane—

THIRRU: I have no money, son—

LILY: He doesn't have a visa, Sid—

SIDDHARTHA: I have money. I can come to Indonesia. And then we can catch a plane, / Appa.

LILY: It's not that simple.

SIDDHARTHA: Don't get on that / boat!

LILY: / Sid …

THIRRU: I'm sorry *mahan*. I'm taking a boat tonight, okay? I must go now—

SIDDHARTHA: I'm coming to Indonesia, Appa.

RADHA: No.

THIRRU: Radha?

SIDDHARTHA: I'll leave in the morning. / I'll be there in two, three days—

LILY: Sid …

RADHA *stands and strikes* SIDDHARTHA *across the face.*

RADHA: You will not!

THIRRU: Radha!

SIDDHARTHA: I have to bring him / here—

RADHA *strikes* SIDDHARTHA *again.*

RADHA: You will not!

SIDDHARTHA: You left him there! / You got on a plane and you left him behind!

RADHA: [*pulling* SIDDHARTHA *away from the phone*] Shut up. You know nothing. / Hang up. Hang up the telephone! Hang up the telephone!

LILY: [*taking* SIDDHARTHA] Sid, listen, / listen to me—

THIRRU: Radha? Radha? எங்க போன்னீங்கள்? (Where were you?) Where were you? எங்க போன்னீங்கள்? (Where were you Radha?) I waited and you never came. I woke up in prison. Twenty-one years I woke up in prison and you never came. Where were you? Who is this boy in Australia who calls me Appa? ராதா? நான் எங்க

இருக்கிறன்? என்ன நடக்குது? எங்க போன்னீங்கள்? ராதா?
Where were you?

RADHA *tries to speak.*

SIDDHARTHA: Amma?

The SMUGGLER *runs to* THIRRU.

SMUGGLER: Come! Now! Now!
THIRRU: ராதா ... நான் என்ன செய்ய? எனக்கு ஒரு வழி சொல்லு
ராதா? (Radha. Tell me. Tell me what to do. Do I come? Yes or no?)

YOUNG RADHA *and* YOUNG THIRRU *enter.*

SIDDHARTHA: Amma?
YOUNG THIRRU: Radha?
YOUNG RADHA: What is the date today?
YOUNG THIRRU: Saturday the twenty-ninth of August.

YOUNG RADHA *and* YOUNG THIRRU *go to the same position that* SIDDHARTHA *and* LILY *stood when they exchanged the date and year in Act One, Scene Two.*

YOUNG RADHA: Saturday the twenty-ninth of August. 1977.

She kisses him tenderly on the cheek.

Saturday the twenty-ninth of August. 1977.

He takes her hands and kisses them gently.

SIDDHARTHA: Amma?

Everyone looks to RADHA. *She nods.*

RADHA: Yes.
SIDDHARTHA: Come, Appa. Amma says come.

Music. Everyone enters. They move across the stage as one.

Ecstatic, SWATHI *yells a Tamil battle cry.*

Terrified, MAITHRI *yells a Sinhala battle cry.*

The SOLDIERS, *the* REFUGEES, SIDDHARTHA, LILY, RADHA *and* THIRRU *are swept into one group.*

THIRRU *is on a crowded boat. The swell of oceans, a storm.*

Wet and desperate, THIRRU *steps forward and speaks to us:*

THIRRU: 'I claim my rights in the Refugee Convention, signed by Australia in 1951, that I have left my country of origin for reasons of persecution. I call upon the Australian Government's spirit of international cooperation to receive my request for asylum and give me an opportunity for resettlement.'

END OF ACT TWO

ACT THREE

SCENE ONE

APAH, *now in his 80s, sits in his chair trying to perfect a Rubik's cube.*

> LILY *waits on Siddhartha's porch. She peers at an image on her phone.*

RADHA *is in her apartment, reading a print out of an online newspaper article.*

SIDDHARTHA *enters, well dressed in a mixture of traditional and western clothing. He's fidgety.* LILY *looks up.*

SIDDHARTHA: Okay.

LILY: Looking good, Mister Eyelashes.

SIDDHARTHA: Thank you.

LILY: You ready?

SIDDHARTHA: Lil' …

LILY: Yeah?

SIDDHARTHA: Why are we here?

LILY: What?

SIDDHARTHA: In Coogee I mean. [*Looking at the audience*] Who are all these people? Like I know Ismet. Hello Ismet.

ISMET: The boy who fixed my Skippy. Son, your mother never replied to my text message.

SIDDHARTHA: No, um, something came up.

ISMET: Quite often a thing will come up. No matter. I remain open to all future possibilities. [*Exiting*] I am an optimist!

SIDDHARTHA: You see, if things had gone a bit differently I might have a Turkish air conditioner installer as a father. Is that how it works? Just like that, everything rearranges? Is that what Sydney is, a lot of rearranged people?

LILY: Sid?

SIDDHARTHA: Something happened to my amma in Sri Lanka in 1983 and so now I'm here. But if whatever that was in 1983 had gone a little bit differently I could be living in a house in Colombo. Or in a refugee camp in India. But I'm not. I'm in Sydney. And I don't know how or why, but I do know that because my amma came here I met you. Now I'm pretty sure I'm in love with you—no I'm definitely sure I'm in love with you—but what I'm also trying to say is that it feels super weird to be in love with you in Coogee. See, in Amma's apartment in Pendle Hill there's a balcony where Ammamma used to sit and teach me thevarams. Like these Tamil lullabies. So I can't speak in Tamil but I can sing in Tamil. It's like an almost-connection. And I'm pretty sure that the chair Amma sits in isn't from Australia. I'm pretty sure it's like the only thing she brought with her from Sri Lanka, and when I sit in it I feel almost connected to … something, and every time I go there the place smells like mustard seeds and curry leaves, and here this place smells like salty air and beer and I love it, I love it Lil', but it's not me, it's not mustard seeds and curry leaves, and Lily if I stay here I think I'm going to become someone else. I thought I wanted to become someone else but I've quite suddenly realised I don't. I need to return to those almost connections before they're gone, and trace them back to where they came from, and actually I'm not sure of any of this at all, I could be completely wrong, I mean my mum's kinda intense and scary and isn't quite aware of fundamental concepts like privacy or mutual respect, but nevertheless Lil'— I think I need to go … home.

LILY: Which means?

SIDDHARTHA: Pendle Hill.

LILY: Uh huh.

SIDDHARTHA: Yeah. And I was hoping that …

LILY: Yeah?

SIDDHARTHA: Maybe— you might like to—

LILY: Move … / in …

SIDDHARTHA: Move in with me …

LILY: And …

SIDDHARTHA: And my amma. No. Yes. Lil'. I think you and I should move in with my amma.

LILY: Uh huh.

SIDDHARTHA: Yep. So. That's it. I'm a bit nervous.

LILY: Okay. Thank you. My turn?

SIDDHARTHA: Yes please.

LILY: It's my nephew's birthday today. My whole family's going hunting. They're having a big cook up. Mud crabs plucked from the mangroves. Yams dug up from near the rivers. Oh my God you need to try these yams Sid. And my nephew! He loves being thrown into the air. He has proper fat cheeks like the Michelin Man. True God!

My family sent me to the city to learn the whitefella way, Sid. That's why I'm studying law. That's why I'm here. It's coz my family sent me to Sydney that I got to meet you. And I'm pretty sure I'm definitely in love with you too.

But in Sydney, I'm a guest. Back home in Yirrkala, on my country, I'm connected through story and knowledge to every clan, every family, every place. It's the oldest conversation I know. And at some point, I'm gonna go back home and I'm gonna continue that conversation. So what do we do about that Siddhartha?

SIDDHARTHA: Okay, okay … Do you think you can have *two* homes?

LILY: Like Sydney and Colombo?

SIDDHARTHA: Or Sydney and Yirrkala?

LILY: Mate that's three already—

SIDDHARTHA: Okay maybe it's not two homes. Maybe it's still one, but just … a bigger one. It expands, you know? When we did the funeral rites for Ammamma, I let her ashes out into the Georges River. Eventually those ashes would have reached the ocean, and somewhere along the line mixed with a river in Yirrkala—

LILY: Or with your mob in Sri Lanka—

SIDDHARTHA: —Exactly.

LILY: Water and water?

SIDDHARTHA: Water and water.

LILY: Everyone gets dragged to the city hey?

SIDDHARTHA: [*he sidles up to her*] Has its advantages.

LILY: Yeah.

> *Beat.*

SIDDHARTHA: I can live up North. I could do Yirrkala.

LILY: Yeah?

SIDDHARTHA: Yes. I'd do anything.

LILY: Thank you.

Beat.

SIDDHARTHA: Wanna try Pendle Hill first?

LILY: It'd be nice to have a Sydney amma. [*Beat.*] Let me think about it, Sid.

SIDDHARTHA: Thank you.

    Beat.

LILY: So are you ready to do this?

SIDDHARTHA: No.

LILY: [*taking his hand*] Come on.

SIDDHARTHA: Okay then. Let's go.

    They exit as Apah's phone rings.

SCENE TWO

NIHINSA *enters with a mat and some chillies. She unfurls it and puts the chillies out to dry.*

RADHA *watches her grandfather.*

APAH *answers the phone.*

APAH: Er— hello? Hello?

HASA: Apah? It's Hasa. [*Beat.*] Sorry Apah— have I woken you?

APAH: [*surprised*] Hasanga? What is it?

HASA: I play cricket with a group of, well, *rowdy* boys …

APAH: Yes?

HASA: You did not hear of any … untoward activities happening last night, did you?

APAH: Where?

HASA: Here. In Colombo.

APAH: In Colombo?! No, why?

HASA: I've heard …

APAH: What have you heard?

HASA: Apparently a few of these cricket boys are planning something.

    YOUNG RADHA *enters. She is four months pregnant. She holds an Amnesty report and other pieces of paper. There is mail waiting for her on her chair.*

Apah?

APAH: Let me check for you, Hasanga.

HASA: Thank you.

APAH: What about Vinsanda? Is he there? Put him on.

HASA: I'm calling from work. Maybe you could try my father at his home? I'm sorry I can't help more, we don't … talk a lot these days.

APAH: I see. [*Beat.*] Call me immediately if you hear anything else.

HASA: Of course.

> APAH *puts the phone down. He thinks. He picks up his address book, trying to find a particular entry.*

YOUNG RADHA: Nihinsa— can we have some tea please? I feel a little nauseous. And could you bring Apah's morning medicine?

> NIHINSA *exits.* YOUNG RADHA *gives* APAH *a piece of paper.*

My shortlist. For the mathematics scholarship.

APAH: Not now darling.

YOUNG RADHA: When you can. I'm sending the list to the staff at Cambridge next week.

APAH: Okay.

YOUNG RADHA: Who was that on the phone?

APAH: Hasanga.

YOUNG RADHA: What did he say?

APAH: Another rumour about some trouble. What is the ayar's number?

> APAH *holds the address book very close to his face. He can't see properly.*

YOUNG RADHA: Here, let me help you with that.

> *She dials the number.*

Are you hungry? I'm starving.

APAH: Not right now.

YOUNG RADHA: I really feel like a cinnamon bun.

> YOUNG RADHA *finishes dialling and hands the phone to him. Then she goes back to her report.*

PRIEST: ஹல்லோ? (Hello?)

APAH: ஐயர்? யார் முத்துவா கதைக்கிறது? (Ayar? Is that you?)

PRIEST: அப்பா [அழுத்தத்துடன்] அப்பிடியெண்டால். … (Apah. [*with gravity*] So.)

APAH: அது தான் உங்களிட்ட கேக்கிறதுக்காவண்டி எடுத்தனான்.
(I was calling to check with you.)

PRIEST: இளம் பெடியளுக்குத்தான் பிரச்சனை எண்டு கேள்விப்படுறன். பெரிசா ஒண்டுமில்ல. நீங்கள் என்ன கேள்விப்படுறீங்கள்? (I've heard only rumours about young boys and some trouble. Nothing substantial. You?)

APAH: கொழும்பிலயும் பிரச்சனயெண்டு ஆக்கள் சொல்லீனம்
(Rumours also, of trouble in Colombo.)

> YOUNG RADHA *looks to* APAH.

PRIEST: / Hmmmm. …

YOUNG RADHA: In Colombo?

APAH: வேற ஏதாவது கேள்விப்பட்டா எடுத்துச் சொல்லுங்கோ என்ன? (Call me if you hear anything else?)

PRIEST: கட்டாயம் (Of course.)

> APAH *puts the phone down.* NIHINSA *enters with tea and Apah's medicine.*

APAH: Darling, dial Vinsanda at home.

YOUNG RADHA: [*dialing*] Have your morning medicine please.

> NIHINSA *offers, but* APAH *stops her.*

APAH: In a moment.

YOUNG RADHA: [*firmly*] Your medicine.

APAH: You are as bad as Aacha was!

> NIHINSA *hands him the medicine.*

Thank you. You know before she passed Aacha taught Nihinsa to read English so she knew exactly what pills I had to take and when— and she made sure the doctor would come and tell her when the prescription changes also.

YOUNG RADHA: Aacha takes care of you even now, no?

APAH: *You* take care of me, Radha.

YOUNG RADHA: [*hanging up the phone*] No answer, Apah.

APAH: Your own parents are out gallivanting across the world making money, but you, you are here. That is why I am leaving this house to you, not them—

YOUNG RADHA: Apah, there's no need to cause mischief. Just let them have / the house—

APAH: Nonsense. It was Aacha's dying wish. You will respect that at least, won't you?

YOUNG RADHA: [*surprised*] Of course.

APAH: What's that you've got there?

YOUNG RADHA: An Amnesty report. In the last six months, at least sixty-five people have been detained under the Prevention of Terrorism Act. Mostly Tamil, but also Singhalese. There are reports of torture. So to help them I'm compiling a list of their names, employment, age, background, and detail of the charges against them.

APAH: Very good.

> YOUNG THIRRU *enters.* NIHINSA *exits.*

YOUNG THIRRU: My love? Feeling any better? Did you have some tea?

YOUNG RADHA: Still feeling pretty icky. I'm having tea, but I don't think it makes any difference.

YOUNG THIRRU: Good morning Apah.

> NIHINSA *enters with tea.*

YOUNG RADHA: [*to* YOUNG THIRRU] I really want one of those cinnamon buns.

YOUNG THIRRU: I'll buy a whole bag of them on the way home! [*To* NIHINSA] ස්තූතියි නිහින්සා (Thank you, Nihinsa.)

YOUNG RADHA: [*opening the mail—there are Polaroid snaps*] Finally! The pictures from the school exchange I organised. The Elpitiya girls on their trip to Jaffna. Their first time in the North!

YOUNG THIRRU: Oh! / This is brilliant!

> *He shows* APAH.

APAH: Well done darling.

NIHINSA: මං ඒ කෙල්ලව දන්නව (I know that girl, Radha bebi.) / Very good!

YOUNG RADHA: They took them to / all the temples—

> *A* FRUIT SELLER *appears at the gate.*

FRUIT SELLER: திரு இருக்கிறாரா? (Is Thirru here?)

YOUNG THIRRU: Ah! That's one of my father's vendors. [*To* FRUIT SELLER] என்ன விஷயம்? (What / is it?)

He goes to him. They whisper.

YOUNG RADHA: [*to* NIHINSA *and* APAH] Once the monsoon season is over we'll bring the Jaffna girls down South. You must meet them, / Nihinsa—

NIHINSA: I'd love to.

APAH: [*to* NIHINSA] This one looks like you!

They laugh.

The FRUIT SELLER *leaves.* YOUNG THIRRU *stands at the gate.*

YOUNG RADHA: Thirru?

YOUNG THIRRU: This fellow says he saw my sister around town. In Jaffna.

Everyone looks at YOUNG THIRRU.

Just for the day. They're recruiting for the Tigers. They're forming a women's wing—

YOUNG RADHA: Yes, I've heard—

YOUNG THIRRU: Apparently the girls seemed very jolly. They seemed … content.

Beat.

Nihinsa Nanda, could you get my lunch please?

NIHINSA *nods and exits.*

Swathi would be twenty-one now. She'd be quite persuasive with the younger ones.

YOUNG RADHA: Thirru—

YOUNG THIRRU: [*firmly*] She's made her choice, Radha. I want nothing to do with it.

Beat. YOUNG THIRRU *feels* YOUNG RADHA*'s belly.*

Any more kicks?

YOUNG RADHA: He gets more active around lunch.

YOUNG THIRRU: You're so sure it's a boy!

YOUNG RADHA: Will you be home late again?

YOUNG THIRRU: Maybe. I'm pitching for that new Chinese construction job today. It could be my big break.

YOUNG RADHA: You know you don't / have to—

YOUNG THIRRU: Yes. I do. [*He looks to* APAH] I need to prove myself—

NIHINSA: Thirru!

YOUNG RADHA: Your lunch!

He gets his lunch from NIHINSA.

YOUNG THIRRU: Get back to that Amnesty report.

YOUNG RADHA: Go get me those cinnamon buns.

YOUNG THIRRU: I love you.

YOUNG RADHA: I love you too.

YOUNG THIRRU: And the little one.

YOUNG RADHA: போயிட்டு வாறன். (See you soon.)

YOUNG THIRRU: போயிட்டு வாங்கோ. (See you soon.)

YOUNG THIRRU *gives* YOUNG RADHA *a peck on the cheek. He exits.*

YOUNG RADHA: And get me some ice cream too! The mango, with fruit and nuts! From Elephant House!

YOUNG THIRRU: [*offstage*] Yes ma'am!

YOUNG RADHA *smiles as she walks back to her chair.* APAH *looks at* YOUNG RADHA *and her smile disappears.*

YOUNG RADHA: Don't.

APAH: I'm concerned for you, darling.

The phone rings.

YOUNG RADHA: Swathi hasn't even talked to Thirru or their parents in years—

APAH: That's not the point!

APAH *picks it up.*

Yes?

PETTAH SHOP OWNER: Apah! So sorry to bother you Sir, you don't know me, I have an imported goods store. The *ayar* gave me / your number—

APAH: Yes? What is / it?

PETTAH SHOP OWNER: We have trouble here—

APAH: Son. Where are you? What is happening?

PETTAH SHOP OWNER: In Pettah. Our shop has just been broken into by hoodlums.

APAH: So call the police!

PETTAH SHOP OWNER: I have. No-one has arrived.

APAH: Wait fifteen minutes. If you have not received help by then, call me.

PETTAH SHOP OWNER: Thank you, Apah.

APAH *hangs up. Then dials the* OPERATOR.

YOUNG RADHA: What's happening? Is this in Colombo?

APAH: Yes. Some trouble in Pettah.

OPERATOR: Operator. How can I help you today Sir?

APAH: Connect me to the officer in charge, Pettah station.

OPERATOR: Putting you through now.

PETTAH POLICE COMMANDER: Pettah Police Commander.

APAH: This is Mannikavasar.

PETTAH POLICE COMMANDER: Apah, how are you today?

APAH: Listen Dilip. There's looting on the main street in Pettah. The victims need police assistance.

PETTAH POLICE COMMANDER: On Main Street? Is that so? Thank you for bringing this to my attention. We'll get control over the situation immediately.

APAH: Dilip—

The line is dead.

APAH *hangs up. Beat.*

YOUNG RADHA: We don't need your concern. Swathi chose one path, we have chosen another.

APAH: It's not that simple Radha. The ayar's nephew joined the Tigers and his son—who has nothing to do with them—lost his job because of it!

YOUNG RADHA: That's the fault of his stupid employers then! Thirru and I have made our position clear, in the family, in public—

APAH: Radha, Thirru's sister is a Tiger! They killed thirteen government soldiers two days ago—

YOUNG RADHA: / I know—

APAH: And they kill other Tamils! That is the group Thirru's sister belongs to—

YOUNG RADHA: You think I don't know this? You know Thirru doesn't support her joining! Thirru has publicly condemned the Tigers, in the community, in the papers. What else can we do?

APAH: Is that supposed to just make everything better?

YOUNG RADHA: Even at our wedding you weren't happy—

APAH: I kept my mouth shut didn't I?

YOUNG RADHA: What a big achievement.

APAH: Why did you do it, darling?

YOUNG RADHA: Excuse me?

APAH: Why did you pick him?

YOUNG RADHA: I love him.

APAH: Kunju, love is not enough.

YOUNG RADHA: Thirru has taught me that listening is more important than being right. Something I could never learn from you, Apah.

The phone rings.

APAH: / Radha—

YOUNG RADHA: That is why I picked him. That is why I love him.

APAH: [*into the phone*] Hello?

WELAWATTE SHOP OWNER: அப்பா … மன்னிக்கோணும் ஐயா. … உங்கள தொந்தரவு செய்யிறதுக்கு மன்னிக்கோணும். (Apah, Sir, so sorry to bother you, you don't know me, the ayar / gave me your—)

APAH: ஓம் ஓம் … இப்ப எங்க இருக்கிறியள் … என்ன நடக்குது அங்க? (Yes yes yes. Where are you and what is happening?)

WELAWATTE SHOP OWNER: வெள்ளவத்தையில அப்பா. காவாலிகள் வந்து எங்கட கடைய உடைச்சப் போட்டாங்கள். கொஞ்சப் பேர், இந்த ரோட்டில இருக்கிற தமிழாக்கள வெருட்டிக் கொண்டு திரியிறாங்கள். (In Welawatte. Hoodlums have ransacked our shop. A few have even begun to threaten Tamils on our street.)

APAH: What?

WELAWATTE SHOP OWNER: Apah?

APAH: யார் தமிழ் எண்டு அவங்களுக்கு எப்பிடித் தெரியும்? (How do they know who is Tamil?)

WELAWATTE SHOP OWNER: ஐடி கார்டை காட்டச் சொல்லிப் பயமுறுத்துறாங்கள். (They bully people into showing their ID cards.)

Beat.

APAH: ஒரு பதினைஞ்சு நிமிஷம் பாருங்கோ. பொலிஸ்

அதுக்குள்ள வரயில்லையெண்டால் (எனக்குத் திரும்ப கோல்
பண்ணுங்கோ) என்னைத் திருப்பிக் கூப்பிடுங்கோ. (Wait
fifteen minutes. Call me again if the police have not arrived by
then.)

WELAWATTE SHOP OWNER: ஓம் அப்பா (Yes Sir.)

  APAH *hangs up and immediately dials the* OPERATOR.

YOUNG RADHA: Apah, you were the one—

APAH: One moment.

OPERATOR: Operator, who do you need?

APAH: Connect me to the IGP.

OPERATOR: One moment.

IGP: Inspector General of Police.

APAH: Chandra. Mannikavasar here.

IGP: Ah yes, Mannikavasar.

APAH: I have reliable reports that Tamil shops are being broken into in
multiple points across the city.

IGP: Yes. We've received other calls on this Apah—

APAH: Is that / so—

IGP: I've instructed my men to be positioned across the city. We'll get
control of the situation, okay Apah?

APAH: I've heard that before.

IGP: Apah?

APAH: Do it now, Chandra.

IGP: Apah, of course.

  APAH *hangs up.*

YOUNG RADHA: Is everything okay?

APAH: He'll take care of it.

YOUNG RADHA: It was you who lent Bala Mama money. You brought
him customers, paid for Thirru's education, let him stay in our
home. Even though he was of a lower caste. You taught me to look
past that.

APAH: Darling. Different castes can mix together. Work together.
But *marriage* is different. Marriage is the coming together of two
families, not just two people. And not for a moment: but forever.

YOUNG RADHA: I know.

APAH: You *can't* know. You're still too young to understand what a long time *feels* like. Why can't you understand that we know what is best for you, because we have been through it already ourselves?

YOUNG RADHA: So that's why history's mistakes are so often repeated.

The phone rings.

APAH: You are unbelievably obstinate.

YOUNG RADHA: It's like looking in a mirror, isn't it?

APAH *picks up the phone.*

APAH: Yes?

KUMARASWAMY: Apah. It's Vasanthi Kumaraswamy here, I was a student of yours many years ago.

APAH: Yes, I remember you Vasanthi.

KUMARASWAMY: I'm now a chair of the city development board, and I work in a building on Galle Rd—

APAH: Very good—

KUMARASWAMY: Sorry Apah. Myself and other state officers, and our families, have been marooned in a building in the middle of the city and are surrounded by hoodlums.

APAH: How serious are they?

Beat.

Are your lives are in peril?

Beat.

Vasanthi!

KUMARASWAMY: I think they're very serious Apah.

APAH: Have you called the police?

KUMARASWAMY: They are here. They brandish guns half-heartedly and laugh at us.

APAH *considers.*

APAH: Do *you* have a weapon?

YOUNG RADHA: / Apah—

KUMARASWAMY: We're civil servants. Even if there was one here— I'm not sure if we—

APAH: I understand. I will do everything I can to send government military personnel that can properly protect you.

KUMARASWAMY: Thank you Apah.

> *He hangs up.*

YOUNG RADHA: What's going on / Apah—

APAH: Call the President.

> YOUNG RADHA *quietens, looks up the name in the book and calls.*

PRESIDENT'S OFFICE: Good Morning. President's Office. How can I help you?

APAH: Mannikavasar here. Get the President on the phone.

> *Pause. The* PRESIDENT *sits next to his* RECEPTIONIST, *dressed for work. He shakes his head.*

Hello?

PRESIDENT'S OFFICE: He's … he's asleep Sir.

APAH: [*to* YOUNG RADHA] What time is it?

YOUNG RADHA: About a quarter past eight, Apah.

APAH: Wake him up. Now.

PRESIDENT'S OFFICE: Okay— but this might take a while—

APAH: I will wait.

> *Pause.*

PRESIDENT: Apah! So good to hear from you. How are you?

APAH: Mister President. Tamil shops and offices are being broken into across Colombo. The local police are not helping the victims. The IGP has not taken action. This has a danger of growing into a full-blown riot. / Do you understand?

YOUNG RADHA: Oh my God …

PRESIDENT: Mister Mannikavasar—

APAH: Mister President, instead of sleeping there, you must move in to the matter. You must send in army personnel to the aid of the victims.

PRESIDENT: Mister Mannikavasar. We have received many reports of this. Rest assured, we are looking into it.

APAH: We must act *now*.

PRESIDENT: I will call the Defence Minister now, okay Apah? We will send in army forces.

APAH: Thank you.

> APAH *hangs up.*

The bloody rascal.

Beat.

Call Vinsanda's office.

YOUNG RADHA *dials.*

YOUNG RADHA: Then I need to call Thirru—
APAH: *Kunju*, first Vinsanda.
YOUNG RADHA: Yes I am, I am. Here.

YOUNG RADHA *passes the phone to* APAH.

JANINI: Hello?
APAH: Janini? It's Apah here. Put Vinsanda on the phone.

Beat.

Janini?
JANINI: Vinsanda told me to clear all his appointments for today, Apah. He's not in his office.
APAH: Then where is he?! No-one is answering his home phone.
JANINI: I don't know Apah. Vinsanda told me he wouldn't be in today. That's all I know.
APAH: [*beat*] Okay, Janini bye.

He goes to hang up.

JANINI: Apah?
APAH: Yes?
JANINI: I'm so sorry.

APAH *considers this as* YOUNG RADHA *takes the phone and dials Thirru's office.*

MAYA: Hello?
YOUNG RADHA: Maya, it's Radha here, is Thirru there?
MAYA: Hello Radha. Of course— I'll put you through.
YOUNG RADHA: Thank God. [*To* APAH] He made it to work.
YOUNG THIRRU: Radha?
YOUNG RADHA: Thirru. There's trouble—
YOUNG THIRRU: I know, I know. People have been calling the office with such stories—
YOUNG RADHA: Stay inside, okay?

YOUNG THIRRU: Absolutely. Radha— I have to go— the phones won't stop ringing, other families are worried too—

YOUNG RADHA: Of course.

YOUNG THIRRU: I'll keep you updated.

YOUNG RADHA: Bye.

YOUNG THIRRU: Bye.

She hangs up.

YOUNG RADHA: Those government soldiers killed in Jaffna by the Tigers. Do you think this is all … retaliation?

APAH: That must have something to do with it. But if it's just a reaction to something that happened only two days ago … It doesn't make sense. This seems too well organised.

The phone rings. APAH *picks it up immediately.*

APAH: Yes?

PETTAH SHOP OWNER: Apah? It's the Pettah shop owner here.

APAH: What is the update?

PETTAH SHOP OWNER: The police have not arrived.

APAH: The army?

PETTAH SHOP OWNER: No-one. Only the mob has gotten bigger.

APAH: To how many?

PETTAH SHOP OWNER: Eight, maybe ten people?

APAH: What, *machaan*! Are you weak? Do you not want to defend yourself?

PETTAH SHOP OWNER: If we use force Apah, it could start trouble …

APAH: Son, clearly there's already trouble!

Beat.

Wait there.

APAH *hangs up.*

Call Arif at his office.

YOUNG RADHA *dials.*

YOUNG RADHA: No-one is hurt yet. If they use violence Apah, won't more violence ensue?

APAH *takes the phone from* YOUNG RADHA.

ARIF: Yes?

APAH: Arif. Apah.

ARIF: / Ah.

APAH: The Tamil shop owner on your street—

ARIF: I can see the mob from my window, Apah.

APAH: And the police?

ARIF: They look on, with grins on their faces.

APAH: What about the Sinhala owned shops on your street?

ARIF: They haven't touched them.

APAH: Are the mob local fellows?

ARIF: No. Definitely not.

APAH: Then how do they know which shops are owned by Tamils?

ARIF: Apah they know.

APAH: But how?

ARIF: That is a dangerous question Apah.

APAH: Arif, I need your help with that shop.

ARIF: I understand. I'll chase the mobs away, *in'sallah.*

> *They hang up.*

APAH: Write this down.

> YOUNG RADHA *writes the following:*

To the Tamil people of Sri Lanka. From this moment on you should take every step to protect your person and property. If you do not have sufficient numbers or adequate strength—

YOUNG RADHA: / Apah—

APAH: —you must immediately evacuate the places where you live or transact business and get into safe Tamil areas.

YOUNG RADHA: / But Colombo is for—

APAH: You must not say thereafter that you were not in a position to be safe; be warned. Signed, Mannikavasar, or— your Apah. Nihinsa!

YOUNG RADHA: What is the need to tell people to flee to *Tamil* areas? Why can't you address *all* Sri Lankans to protect each other?

APAH: Do you not see what is happening, Radha?

YOUNG RADHA: If you cross this line, Apah, you will not be able to go back.

APAH: It has been crossed, and not by us!

YOUNG RADHA: Us, them— there can be no separation, no violence.

APAH: When you are secure you can fight for equality. But when you are no longer safe you can only fight for your survival.

YOUNG RADHA: [*waving the paper*] This is not Sri Lanka!

APAH: In Urumpirai, our ancestral village, we are famous for our special brand of pot arrack.

YOUNG RADHA: What are you talking about / Apah—

APAH: Shut up and listen. In the old days toddy was freely available. It was given to mothers for post-natal nourishment. They never became *intoxicated*. Then the British put through the toddy regulations law and it changed the culture. Arrack became something manufactured and expensive. Toddy booths, arrack taverns, *rasayanam* and *kasipu* sprung up everywhere. People got *drunk* from it. But our village was different, Radha. We decided *not* to obey the law. When the European regulation parties found out, they personally came and interrupted arrack preparations on the ground, intruding on our way of life. Our entire village stood up for itself. As a boy I watched your Aacha's mother lead the village women to summarily break pots over the heads of these men and drive them back to their cities. We considered it our *birthright* to make the stuff our way. It was in Urumpirai that I first learnt the rudiments of democracy. Democracy means the *counting* of heads, within certain limits, and the *cracking* of heads beyond those limits. To *this day*, our village holds its reputation intact— and the arrack is still smuggled to Madras, where it is in great demand.

YOUNG RADHA: Gandhiji held his reputation intact without breaking a pot over anyone's head.

APAH: We are not all Ghandiji, Radha. Most probably, no-one ever will be again. [*Beat*] නිහින්සා, මේක අරන් පාර උඩහ සිවනන්දන්ගේ ගෙදරට ගිහින් එයාගේ අතටම බාරදෙන්න. මේ ලිපිය, වහාම ටෙලිග්‍රෑම් කරන්න කියන්න හැම ප්‍රධාන පත්තරේකටම ... රේඩියෝ, ටීවී චැනල් හැම එකකටම ... අපේ ලයිස්තුවේ ඉන්න හැම දෙමළ කණ්ඩායම් නායකයෙකුටම. හුඟක් හදිස්සී කියන්න. යන්න! (Nihinsa! Take this statement of mine and go to Sivanandan's house just up the road. Tell him to telegram this message to every major Tamil newspaper, radio and TV station and to every Tamil community leader in our database as a matter of urgency. *Go*!)

NIHINSA *takes the letter and exits.*

The phone rings. YOUNG RADHA *answers.*

YOUNG THIRRU: Radha!

YOUNG RADHA: Love? Are they near you?

YOUNG THIRRU: They've already passed through—

YOUNG RADHA: Thank God.

YOUNG THIRRU: They came up to our office and demanded the Tamil workers. My colleagues told them that there were no Tamils here, and then they took scissors and rulers and blocks of wood and pushed them in the mob's faces and the mob left. I'm alright. I'm going to be alright.

>   YOUNG RADHA *is too relieved to speak.*

Radha?

YOUNG RADHA: Yes?

YOUNG THIRRU: If something happens today, and we can't call each other— let's meet in the little mechanics shed, behind Saraswathi Lodge. You remember?

YOUNG RADHA: Your cousin's shed.

YOUNG THIRRU: Yes.

>   *Beat.*

Are you okay?

YOUNG RADHA: Yes. So, you'll stay inside the office?

YOUNG THIRRU: For now. I'll come back home as soon as it's safe to do so. I love you, Radha.

YOUNG RADHA: I love you too.

>   *She hangs up.*

APAH: We are moving back to Jaffna.

YOUNG RADHA: Absolutely not. I will stay in Colombo.

APAH: Don't be stupid, Radha.

YOUNG RADHA: No. I will stay with my countrymen, not my race. They saved Thirru.

>   *The phone rings.* APAH *answers.*

APAH: Yes?

WELAWATTE SHOP OWNER: அப்பா.. நான் இன்னும்

வெள்ளவத்தையில தான் நிக்கிறன். பொலிஸ்காரன் ஒருத்தரும் இன்னும் வரயில்ல. காவாலிகளிண்ட சண்டித்தனம் கூடிக்கொண்டே போகுது. (Sir, I'm in Welawatte. No-one has arrived. The hoodlums are becoming increasingly violent, they're harassing my staff …)

> *Beat.*

APAH: Yes?

WELAWATTE SHOP OWNER: நீங்கள் ஒம் எண்டு சொன்னா. … நாங்கள், நாங்கள் யாரெண்டத அவங்களுக்குக் காட்டுவம் அப்பா. (With permission Sir, I can teach these hooligans the lesson of their lives.)

APAH: கையில என்ன கிடைக்குதோ அதால அவங்கள போட்டு சாத்துங்கோ. (Lay it thick on them with whatever you have.)

> APAH *hangs up. They look at the phone, but it does not ring.* NIHINSA *returns.*

YOUNG RADHA: If they defend themselves with violence Apah, won't more violence ensue?

APAH: What are the options Radha?

YOUNG RADHA: I will call ten, twenty people—Tamil and Singhalese— and we will go into the middle of Colombo and fast, unto our deaths if necessary. Imagine the attention we would get, in the community, all over the country. The whole world would sit up and take notice—

APAH: Do you know those twenty people Radha?

YOUNG RADHA: / I— yes I could—

APAH: Would *you* lead them by example?

YOUNG RADHA: / I—

APAH: Even *if* the whole world took notice: they wouldn't *act* upon it. What do we know of the struggle of other people around the world? Who do we really care for, but our own?

> *The phone rings.*

We cannot look to the world for help, darling. Today, we cannot even look to our own government.

> APAH *answers.*

PRIEST: Apah. We have a situation here—

APAH: *Ayar*? What is it?

PRIEST: A Tamil man was set alight on Galle Rd, and—

APAH: / —my God.

PRIEST: A few incensed Tamil youth have pulled a Buddhist monk out onto the street and are threatening to set him alight as revenge—

APAH: You can see this? You can see them setting the monk alight?

YOUNG RADHA: / *Mooroha*—

PRIEST: From my window.

APAH: Get out. Run screaming into their midst telling them to stop. Become *livid*. Then fake a heart attack. *Die, Ayar.* Fake your own death in the middle of the crowd. Those young men will run away.

PRIEST: Very well then.

APAH: Go!

He hangs up.

YOUNG RADHA: You order the shop owners to defend themselves— and then tell the *ayar* to stop these other men from taking the same initiative?

The phone rings.

APAH: What did that monk do to anyone?

YOUNG RADHA *nods.* APAH *answers.*

KUNTHAVI: Aiyo, Apah! It's Kunthavi here. Mobs are marching down our street!

APAH: What?! [*To* RADHA] It's Kunthavi Mami. The mobs are on her street.

YOUNG RADHA: / On Jaya Rd?!

APAH *nods.* YOUNG RADHA *and* NIHINSA *walk to the front gates and look outside.*

KUNTHAVI: The hooligans are going to every Tamil house and ransacking the place! One has been burnt to the ground! Our house is next—

APAH: Get out of there *immediately*. Go to your brother's place!

YOUNG RADHA: [*rushing back*] Apah! There's no time. Tell her to go to her neighbours!

KUNTHAVI: Nowhere that is Tamil in Colombo is safe anymore, Apah.

APAH: …

YOUNG RADHA *takes the phone.*

YOUNG RADHA: Kunthavi? It's Radha here. Do you have a neighbour who is not Tamil that you can trust?

KUNTHAVI: I— Yes. Yes I do, Radha darling.

YOUNG RADHA: Go—all of you there—and ask to stay in their house. Now!

KUNTHAVI: Okay. Okay. We'll go right away.

YOUNG RADHA *hangs up. She starts dialling another number.*

YOUNG RADHA: Nihinsa! ඇඳුම් ටිකක් දාගන්න. යන්න ලෑස්ති වෙන්න. පාර පල්ලෙහා ගුනතිලකලගේ ගෙදරට යමු— ඒගොල්ලෝ සිංහල. එහෙ යටමාලයක් තියෙනවා. (Pack some bags. Get ready to leave. We can go to the Goonetillike house down the road—they're Sinhala. They have a basement.)

NIHINSA: හොඳයි බේබි (Yes Maami.)

No-one answers. She hangs up.

YOUNG RADHA: [*whispers*] Thirru!

The phone rings. She pounces on it.

Hello?

HASA: Hello? It's Hasa. Is Apah there?

YOUNG RADHA *gives* APAH *the phone.*

YOUNG RADHA: Hasa.

APAH: Hasanga?! Yes, tell me. Quickly.

HASA: I managed to contact that cricket friend—

APAH: Speak up, I can hardly hear you—

HASA: I'm calling from a public telephone—

APAH: Why on earth—

HASA: I'm taking pictures on the street.

APAH: Hasa—

HASA: Apah. Listen. I don't know if this is true, but my cricket friend. He works for the government. And he said he knew that hooligans would not be punished by the police today.

APAH: He knew that early this morning?

HASA: Apparently.

APAH: You may have trouble getting those photos published, / Hasa.

HASA: They've stopped a bus in the middle of the street. It's packed full of Tamil passengers. They're pouring petrol over it Apah!

Offstage, many hooligans yell 'demala' and other derogatory terms.

APAH: / Hasa?

HASA: / [*running offstage*] ඒයි! පිස්සුද ? නවත්තපල්ලා ! කියන දේ අහලා ඕක නවත්තපල්ලා ! (Hey! Idiot! Stop it! Stop it I said!)

APAH: / Hasa?! [*Yelling*] Hasa?! / I'm coming there now, I'm coming there Hasa—

YOUNG RADHA: Hang up the phone Apah! Hang it up! Hang it up!

YOUNG RADHA grabs the phone and hangs it up. Pause. Total silence.

APAH: Two languages, one country. One language, two countries.

Pause.

NIHINSA returns with packed bags.

VINSANDA enters.

Beat.

YOUNG RADHA: Vinsanda Mama.

APAH and VINSANDA stare at each other.

APAH: Did you know?

Pause.

Did you know?!

Pause.

VINSANDA: You are safe here. Stay at home. Do not leave.

VINSANDA exits.

APAH, shocked, hangs his head in shame. YOUNG RADHA dials YOUNG THIRRU again.

YOUNG RADHA: Nihinsa. Pack my papers up please.

NIHINSA does. No-one answers the phone. YOUNG RADHA hangs up.

A MESSENGER *knocks on the gates.*

MESSENGER: මේ මාණික්කවාසර්ගෙ ගෙදරද? (Is this the Mannikavasar house?)

NIHINSA: ඔව්? (Yes?)

He gives a piece of paper to NIHINSA.

MESSENGER: රාධා සිවකුමාර්ට පණිවිඩයක් තියෙනව. (Message for Radha Sivakumar.)

He exits.

NIHINSA *hands the paper to* YOUNG RADHA.

NIHINSA: බේබි, මේක මායා කියලා නෝන්නා කෙනෙක් දෙන්න කිව්වා ... තිරූ මහත්තයගෙ ඔපිස් එකෙන් කිව්වා (Maya sent this to you Radha. From Thirru's office.)

YOUNG RADHA *reads the note. The phone rings. She pounces on it.*

OPERATOR: [*agitated*] Ma'am!

YOUNG RADHA: I'm here. I'm here.

OPERATOR: Sorry if that upset you. I'm fielding so many calls today. The woman who wants to patch through to you is highly emotional—

YOUNG RADHA: Please put the woman through. උදව්කරාට (Thank you) Thank you for helping us.

OPERATOR: නැතුව කොහොමද ... මෙහෙම වෙලාවට ... (Of course. We have to help each other in times like this.) I have an urgent call for you from Australia. May I put it through?

YOUNG RADHA: From Australia? [*Beat*] Okay. Yes.

OPERATOR: Connecting you now.

DHAMAYANTHI: Radha?!

YOUNG RADHA: Amma—

DHAMAYANTHI: Are you safe?

YOUNG RADHA: Yes—

DHAMAYANTHI: Thank God. I've been trying to call you but the phone has been engaged the whole time! What on earth has been going on there?

YOUNG RADHA: Apah has been fielding a lot of calls—

DHAMAYANTHI: Radha listen. It is not safe for you to stay in / Sri Lanka—

YOUNG RADHA: [*looking at the note*] Amma I have to / go—

DHAMAYANTHI: Listen to me! I've asked Hasa to organise humanitarian visas for you all, to come to Australia. Stay in the house and wait for him to bring them / over.

YOUNG RADHA: / Amma—

DHAMAYANTHI: Is Thirru with you?

YOUNG RADHA: [*looking at the note*] No …

DHAMAYANTHI: Where is he then? [*Beat*] Radha? Radha!

YOUNG RADHA: [*looking at the note*] Thirru has disappeared. Maya says that government officials came to their building this afternoon. Asking for Thirru. They named Swathi. His sister. They named the Tigers.

DHAMAYANTHI: *Moorooha, / Ganesha*—

YOUNG RADHA: I have to /go—

DHAMAYANTHI: I was hoping he had somehow made it back home to you, but if not, / Radha—

YOUNG RADHA: Amma I know exactly where he is. He's hiding out the back of Saraswathi Lodge. I'll go get him / now—

DHAMAYANTHI: *Do not leave the house*! Thirru is very dangerous! You said they mentioned Swathi by name? I told you that whole family are dangerous. Are you listening? It is not safe for you to remain in Sri Lanka!

YOUNG RADHA: Thirru is safe. I'll find him—

DHAMAYANTHI: You are not listening! Listen! It is highly unlikely that Thirru is alive anymore. Whether he is or not it is too dangerous for you to stay in Sri Lanka. Probably more dangerous for you if he is alive. You said they asked for him by name, Radha. Are you listening?

YOUNG RADHA: … Yes.

DHAMAYANTHI: You may do what you wish with your own life, but not with Siddhartha's. That child is not just Thirru's child. That is our child too. Pack your bags. Stay in the house. Wait for Hasa. And Radha? When you do leave, do not wear your *pootu* or *thali* okay? Just act … invisible.

> YOUNG RADHA *holds a finger to the pootu that sits between her eyes.*

DHAMAYANTHI: Radha? Are you listening?

> YOUNG RADHA *hangs up the phone.*
>
> *Pause.*
>
> *She hesitates with her pootu, but doesn't take it off.*
>
> *She walks to the gates.*

YOUNG RADHA: Nihinsa. Call the driver.

> NIHINSA *is with* APAH.

NIHINSA: Radha *bebi* …

> APAH *is not moving.*

SCENE THREE

Music and fire. Loud, rhythmic drums.

RADHA *stands up and begins to change into a saree. It is the same saree that* YOUNG RADHA *is wearing.*

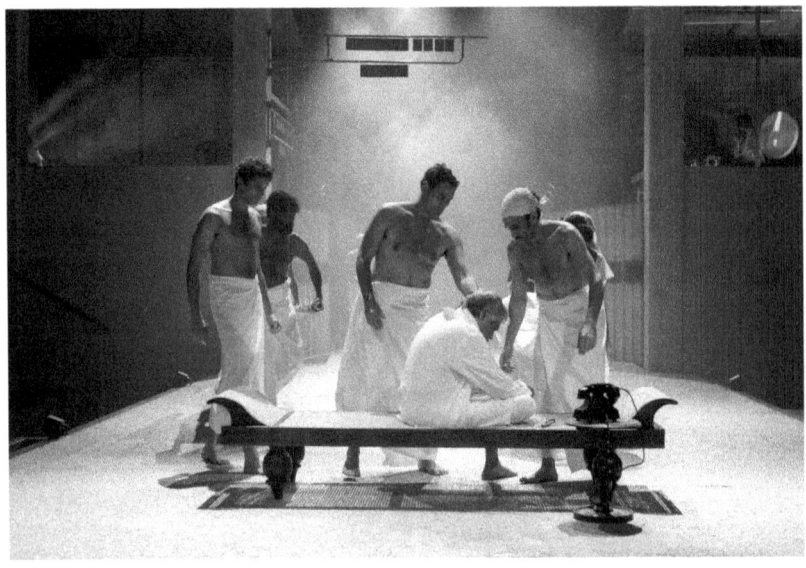

Left to right: Shiv Palekar, Antonythasan Jesuthasan, Nicholas Brown, Prakash Belawadi and Hazem Shammas in the Belvoir/Co-Curious production. Photo: Brett Boardman.

A funeral procession. The PRIEST *enters, chanting.* RADHA *drapes garlands around* APAH*'s body.* HASA *and several other men of different Sri Lankan cultural backgrounds enter and carry* APAH*'s body out on a bamboo platform.*

Low drumming.

HASA *remains.*

YOUNG RADHA *sits unmoving in* AACHA*'s chair.*

HASA: Saraswathi Lodge has been burnt down to the ground. The entire area—the college, the market—is in flames—mobs are everywhere.

    Beat.

Your mother rang again.

    YOUNG RADHA *shakes her head.*

HASA: I have the visa for you.

    YOUNG RADHA *shakes her head. She stands up and moves to the gates.*

NIHINSA: එළියට නං යන්න එපා (You can't go outside—)

    The noise of a homemade explosive. YOUNG RADHA *sits down again.*

    Wild drumming.

    Low drumming.

    YOUNG RADHA *still sits unmoving.*

    RADHA *continues to drape the saree.*

    HASA *and the* PRIEST *are there.*

    The PRIEST *holds a Tupperware box with Apah's ashes. He gives the box to* YOUNG RADHA.

PRIEST: நான் கெதியில செய்ய வேண்டியதாப் போச்சு, ஆனா ஒழுங்காத் தான் செய்தனான். கோயிலுக்குப் பின்னால, ஒதுக்குப் புறமா … தனியா. இனி களனி கங்கை பக்கமா நடந்து பாப்பம், மிச்சத்த முடிக்கலாமா எண்டு. (I had to rush, but I did the proper ceremony. In the back of the temple, in private. Now we could try to walk down to the Kelani river and complete it …)

YOUNG RADHA *stands up.*

HASA *is at the gates.*

HASA: Ssssh. … There is a body on the street.

Everyone pauses.

There are men. [*Beat.*] A Buddhist monk is pointing to this house. [*Beat.*] නිහිංසා දොරවල් වහලා අගුලු දාන්න (Nihinsa lock the doors.)

NIHINSA: පුලුවන්ද මන්දා . .... මෙහෙ කවදාවත් දොරේ අගුල් දාලා නෑ (I don't know if that's possible …)

YOUNG RADHA: We have never locked these doors.

HASA *runs out into the street.*

HASA: [*offstage*] පලයන් යන්න! අඩිය තියන් නෑ මේ ගෙදරට! මෙහෙ මොකුත් නෑ උඹලට ! පලයන් යන්න! (You rascals! Get away from this house! There's nothing for you here— go! *Go!!!*)

PRIEST: Another time, Radha. Another time.

Wild drumming.

Low drumming.

YOUNG RADHA *sits in the chair.*

RADHA *continues to drape the saree.*

HASA: Radha. Mobs have been rioting throughout Colombo for seven days now—despite the curfew. They have crowbars and kitchen knives. Tamil homes, shops, streets are on fire. There are refugee camps set up around the city but I can't find Thirru anywhere. Now there's so many refugees the government is shipping them up North. The army and navy have started firing on a building in the city centre with machine guns. Supposedly there's Tamil Tigers inside. There's violence in Nuwaraya Eliya. Kandy a few days ago.

Beat.

I have the visa if you want it.

YOUNG RADHA *doesn't respond.*

Wild drumming.

Low drumming.

YOUNG RADHA *sits with the ashes on her lap and the phone to her ear.*

RADHA *continues to drape the saree.*

DHAMAYANTHI: There are four thousand people who want these visas, Radha. The Australian Government has set a limit of just over a hundred. If you don't take it, someone else—

YOUNG RADHA *hangs up.*

HASA: Swathi is dead. The police called Bala and he identified her body in Vavuniya. I've called or visited every jail cell and camp in Colombo, Radha. [*Pause.*] I will keep looking for Thirru. [*Beat.*] But Radha … I will be looking for a body.

Beat.

I will come back tomorrow.

HASA *exits.*

Pause.

RADHA *has finished dressing and watches the following closely.*

SUNIL: [*offstage*] Hello? Helloooooo?

NIHINSA *looks to* YOUNG RADHA. *She shakes her head.*

NIHINSA *exits.*

You have nothing to worry about. I'm separated from all this.

NIHINSA: [*offstage*] අනේ එපා ... සර් (No, please, Sir—)

SUNIL: I know my own way in this house, I have been here …

SUNIL *enters.* NIHINSA *is a few steps behind.*

Before. *Vannakam.* My name is Sunil, madam.

He extends his hand.

Beat.

YOUNG RADHA *does not take it.*

Ah yes. Not big on handshakes. I remember. We've met before. At a wedding in this very house. It was brief. I know your grandfather a bit better—nothing like that, nothing like that. You don't have to worry about me. I'm separated from all this, cleeeeanly separated. I'm from India, here on business only—

*Left to right: Vaishnavi Suryaprakash and Nadie Kammallaweera in the
Belvoir/Co-Curious production. Photo: Brett Boardman.*

YOUNG RADHA: My grandfather is dead.

SUNIL: I'm very sorry to hear that Radha. But I'm not here about your grandfather. You see, I'm interested in buying your house. I heard that you might be interested in selling it?

Beat.

Is your husband here? Perhaps I could chat to him— Thirru? I remember him well, very honourable fellow.

YOUNG RADHA: No.

SUNIL: Oh?

Pause.

NIHINSA: කියන්න එපා බේබි (Podi nona, don't tell him.)

Beat.

YOUNG RADHA: My husband is dead.

Beat.

SUNIL: Oh. I am sorry to hear that, Radha. Truly.

Beat.

Shall I talk to your parents?

YOUNG RADHA: They're not in Sri Lanka.

SUNIL: I see.

Beat.

And when do you *leave*?

Beat.

YOUNG RADHA: My visa offer will expire at the end of the week.

SUNIL: I could give you cash. [*Beat.*] This afternoon, if you like.

Long pause. RADHA *shakes her head.*

YOUNG RADHA: Okay.

SUNIL: Sorry, madam?

NIHINSA: [*in shock*] Radha *bebi*?

YOUNG RADHA: Take it. I need to sell it.

SUNIL: Very good. I will give you a fair price. I promise.

A number of people enter and take everything off the stage. It is empty now save for the actors.

YOUNG RADHA *gives her jewellery to a distraught* NIHINSA *and pushes her away.* NIHINSA *exits.*

If you don't mind me asking, where are you going?

Beat.

YOUNG RADHA: Australia.
SUNIL: All the way over there?

SCENE FOUR

RADHA *sits on a train.*

YOUNG RADHA, *still holding the Tupperware container with Apah's ashes, sits on a plane.*

Silence.

The routine, background sounds of travel.

YOUNG RADHA *exits as* SIDDHARTHA *and* LILY *enter.*

SIDDHARTHA: I said we'd meet her on the last carriage of the train …
LILY: There.

SIDDHARTHA *and* LILY *sit beside* RADHA.

SIDDHARTHA: Hello, Amma.
LILY: Hi Radha Amma.

Silence. Then RADHA *speaks.*

RADHA: We lived on Milagiriya Avenue. In Colombo. In a house your great-grandfather built. Our neighbours were Arif Mama and Salwa Mami. During Ramadan, every night, they would bring over food and your great-grandmother and Nihinsa would serve a small feast in their honour. Everyone gathered on our porch: not just Arif and Salwa, but also our dear friends the Goonetillekes, the Van Landenbergs and Kunthavi Mami from the down the road. Even Bala: the fruit seller from Jaffna. [*Beat*] That was Sri Lanka. That was my Ceylon.

Your great-grandparents built a home … a whole world around us. They protected us within its walls. Growing up, I thought we were—and that it was—indestructible.

But it wasn't. What we had built was fragile—so fragile, and it was being worn down, brick by brick, until one day people were turning around and killing the person on their left, or their right … the person in front or behind you …

Then Hasa told me your father too was dead and I … It was like the air itself had became poison. How could Sri Lanka do this to me? The country had broken my heart.

When I got on that plane to Australia, I promised myself that I would protect you. That I would build walls so high around you that we would be indestructible again.

Beat.

But I can't. I can't protect you.

Pause. RADHA *gives* SIDDHARTHA *the article print out.*

Siddhartha. This article was published in the *Leader* newspaper today in Sri Lanka. Read it. / And for God's sake don't—

SIDDHARTHA: / But why?

RADHA: / —ask me why. *Listen.* This article, from the main independent paper in Sri Lanka, was written by the man who freed your father.

SIDDHARTHA: Thirru was freed by a journalist?

RADHA: Read the article.

SIDDHARTHA: It's by a man called … [*He struggles with the name*] 'Hasanga.'

HASA *enters.*

Over the next few minutes, each of the other cast members also enter, one by one, and stand around RADHA, SIDDHARTHA *and* LILY. *Only* THIRRU *does not.*

RADHA: [*pronouncing it properly*] Hasanga.

SIDDHARTHA: Hasanga.

RADHA: We used to call him Hasa.

SIDDHARTHA: Hasa. I spoke to him. On the phone.

RADHA: … yes.

SIDDHARTHA: Amma?

RADHA: Read it, Siddhartha.

SIDDHARTHA *reads.*

HASA: 'No other profession calls on its practitioners to lay down their lives save the armed forces and, in Sri Lanka, journalism. Our stories serve as a mirror in which the public can see itself without make-up or styling gel. From us you learn the state of your nation.'

SIDDHARTHA *stops and looks up at* RADHA.

RADHA: Go on.

HASA: 'In the course of the past few years, countless journalists have been harassed, threatened and killed. It has been my honour to belong to all those categories and now especially the last.'

SIDDHARTHA: Is he saying—

RADHA: Two nights ago Hasa was hit many times in a drive-by shooting. I've called his family and sent our condolences.

SIDDHARTHA: Today?

RADHA: You know Siddhartha, I do all sorts of things before you even wake up. Keep reading.

HASA: 'Why do we do it? After all, I have friends. I have family. Is it worth the risk? Many people tell me it is not.

LILY: Villawood Station.

They stand and walk.

HASA: 'But there is a calling that is above high office, fame, money or security. It is the call of conscience.'

RADHA: This is where Hasa and I differ. One of Apah's batch mates was Hasa's father, Vinsanda. As they grew older, Apah started calling Vinsanda his PF/PE—'personal friend, political enemy.'

Beat.

It is possible to give too much to your country. I saw it happen to your Apah. Now it's happened to Hasa too.

SIDDHARTHA: You mean what happened to Hasa, happened to Apah as well?

Beat.

RADHA: Siddhartha. Apah's ashes have been sitting under my bed for twenty-one years. I want you to come to Sri Lanka to help me finish the funeral rites for him. After that, perhaps I will tell you the story of your great-grandfather.

LILY: Villawood Detention Centre.

They stop. All actors are on stage except THIRRU.

RADHA *doesn't move.*

RADHA: I was one of the lucky ones.

Beat.

I loved Sri Lanka. I still do. Not just the people, but the land itself. I miss it. Every day.

Beat.

You know, if I had stayed for just one more week—I might never have left. Most probably I would not have left …

SIDDHARTHA: What?

RADHA: [*she reaches out to touch her son's face*] If not for you.

Pause.

Come.

They step forward.

They scan the faces for THIRRU.

Way up the back …

LILY: Amma. Siddhartha.

RADHA *looks straight across at* THIRRU.

RADHA: That's your father, Siddhartha.

THIRRU *walks over to his family.*

They embrace.

The entire cast stand together. They walk to the front of the stage and bow to the audience.

THE END

ALSO AVAILABLE FROM CURRENCY PRESS

Lighten Up by Nicholas Brown and Sam McCool

In Australia, we like 'em blonde and bronzed. In India, it's 'fair and lovely'. So what happens if you're stuck in between?

John Green is an Anglo-Indian Australian actor who dreams of being cast in his favourite TV soap, 'Bondi Parade'. The problem is, his coloured contacts can't hide the fact that his skin is more brown than white.

Meanwhile, his skin-bleached mum is determined for him to procreate with a blonde, white Aussie woman in order to rid the family of any sign of their ethnic heritage. All hell breaks loose when John falls in love with an Indigenous woman called Sandy.

This very funny play by actor (and Bollywood leading-man) Nicholas Brown and comedian Sam McCool tells a universal tale of identity, cultural assimilation and bleaching your bits.

ISBN 9781760620288   PB

The Drover's Wife by Leah Purcell

Tarantino meets *Deadwood* in this full-throttle drama of our colonial past, written by the indomitable Leah Purcell.

Henry Lawson's story of the drover's wife pits the stoic silhouette of a woman against the unforgiving Australian landscape, staring down a serpent—it's our frontier myth captured in a few pages. In Purcell's new play the old story gets a very fresh rewrite. Once again the drover's wife is confronted by a threat in her yard in Australia's high country, but now it's a man. He's bleeding, he's got secrets, and he's black. She knows there's a fugitive wanted for killing whites, and the district is thick with troopers, but something's holding the drover's wife back from turning this fella in…

A taut thriller of our pioneering past, *The Drover's Wife* is full of fury, power and has a black sting to the tail, reaching from our nation's infancy into our complicated present.

ISBN 9781760620974   PB

Staging Asylum: Contemporary Australian Plays About Refugees by Emma Cox (Ed)

'While the theatre stands up for the despised, Australian culture and decency are not yet dead.' — Thomas Keneally

The first of its kind, this timely anthology brings together six contemporary Australian plays that offer a range of narratives and perspectives on asylum seekers. A vexed issue within the Australian community—particularly among politicians, who often use asylum seekers to further their own ends—this collection contributes to Australia's ongoing discourse on unauthorised asylum seekers, immigration detention, border control and the right to belong.

This eclectic collection includes *CMI (A Certain Maritime Incident)* by version 1.0, a smart, ironic verbatim work that deals with the Children Overboard Affair and the SIEV X disaster; *The Rainbow Dark* by Victoria Carless, a surreal domestic satire about immigration detention; *The Paci ic Solution* by Ben Eltham, which takes armchair cricket commentary as a point of departure for a farce about the Howard government's excision of migration territory; *Halal-el-Mashakel* by Linda Jaivin, which looks at the friendship between two detained asylum seekers; *Journey of Asylum–Waiting* devised by Catherine Simmonds, a series of vignettes based upon the personal experiences of asylum seekers and refugees living in Melbourne; and *Nothing But Nothing* by Towfiq Al-Qady, an autobiographical play about childhood and war.

With a main Introduction as well as separate introductions to each play by editor and drama lecturer Dr Emma Cox, *Staging Asylum* recognises the crucial role that theatre has played—and continues to play—in one of Australia's most hotly debated and urgent contemporary issues.

ISBN 9780868199832   PB

Melbourne Talam by Rashma N Kalsie

'I have completely lost my talam. All I hear is the ring of mobile phones, the noise of escalators, platform announcements and the trains squealing on the tracks. Where's the koyal, where's the ring of temple bells, where's Carnatic music, where's my mother's voice?'

Three young people see each other across a crowded Flagstaff station. They just missed the train. Now they wait. And think. They think about home: Punjab, Delhi, Hyderabad. And about how they just can't seem to get Melbourne's rhythm right. And of all the impossible things they must do to stay. And their time is running out.

Developed through MTC CONNECT and the NEON and Cybec Electric play development programs, this vibrant play puts Melbourne's contemporary social issues at centre stage.

ISBN 9781760620851   PB

Acts of Courage: Three Headphone Verbatim Plays by Roslyn Oades

Acts of Courage forges immediacy and honesty between a vast range of Australian stories, generating forgiveness and hope in the act. Oades' unwavering loyalty to the words, sounds and silences of everyday conversations conveys a steadfast loyalty to the experiences and the people from which they come. This trilogy celebrates not only the Australian spirit through times of hardship, but everyday, extraordinary, acts of courage.

Stories of Love and Hate was made in response to the 2005 Cronulla Riots. It traces the lives and loves of the passionate people who were there.

In *Fast Cars and Tractor Engines*, ordinary people tell extraordinary stories about the fight of their lives as cultures collide, punches are dodged and youthful confessions of love are shared.

Set in a boxing ring, *I'm Your Man* explores notions of masculinity, courage and respect.

ISBN 9781925005257   PB

www.currency.com.au

Visit Currency Press' website now to:

- Buy your books online
- Browse through our full list of titles, from plays to screenplays, books on theatre, film and music, and more
- Choose a play for your school or amateur performance group by cast size and gender
- Obtain information about performance rights
- Find out about theatre productions and other performing arts news across Australia
- For students, read our study guides
- For teachers, access syllabus and other relevant information
- Sign up for our email newsletter

Printed in the USA
CPSIA information can be obtained
at www.ICGtesting.com
CBHW061549061024
15371CB00053B/1705